SIMPLE
SUCCESS
STRATEGIES

LIVE THE LIFE YOU DESERVE

DELORES CRUM

Simple Success Strategies: Live the Life You Deserve

Copyright © 2021 Delores Crum

For more information, email delores@delorescrum.com

Paperback ISBN: 978-1-7366248-0-7

Contents

With a grateful heart, thank you, Richard, for everything.

For our children and grandchildren, and generations to follow.
May your lives be enriched by the message in this book.
I love you all beyond measure.

Acknowledgements

My daughter, Angela Smith Nussel, deserves my deepest gratitude for her help with this work—and for so much more! Her support was essential and her insights invaluable.

Thank you to my Premiere Events and Party Times teams. Their professionalism, expertise, and care for our customers enabled me to focus on completing this work.

I'm grateful for my events industry colleagues and associates—they set the bar high. Their competence and caring help elevate us all.

Thank you to the not-for-profit groups and organizations, along with the various trade associations, who've allowed me to be a part of your important work. Whether as an officer, board/committee member or time, talent and "treasure" contributor, my life, and our family, have been enriched by our service.

Heartfelt appreciation to Team SSS. Thank you for your thoughts and opinions, and for your contributions to this work. You all rock!

Jaclyn Reuter, River Valley Publishing, edited this book, and Margarita Felix, 100 Covers, designed the cover. Many thanks, ladies. Thank you, Michelle Chavez Lazarz, for your contributions and manuscript improvements.

My apologies in advance for any errors in this manuscript that may have escaped my scrutiny and survived the editing process. Any errors are solely my responsibility. I hope that any fault you may find does not affect your enjoyment of this book or dilute the message

Prologue

MANY BOOKS ARE WRITTEN by highly successful men and women whose stories you've heard and whose names you know. Some authors are household names, renowned for the fortunes they've amassed, the heights they've reached, or the influence they exert. Their achievements are widely celebrated and their accomplishments impressive. That's not this book.

This book was written by a person who shares your struggles, battles the same insecurities, and who faces, or who has faced, many of the same issues and challenges that you do. By an individual whose father sold used cars for a living and whose stay-at-home mom fit the 1960s homemaker mold. By a woman raised in a barely middle-class Oklahoma suburb, to a family that sometimes struggled to make ends meet. By a life-long-learner, and my family's first college graduate.

This book will reveal more of my story, and along the way, provide insights and perspectives based on personal experience, observation, and research. It's my hope that you'll find this book imminently relatable. My story could be yours—or anyone's. I learned many life lessons from an early first marriage and, after having two (truly wonderful) children, a divorce. In my second marriage, I found my true soul mate. Surely, in the grand scheme, we were destined to be together!

I've experienced the challenges of helping establish a blended family. Over the years, our tribe grew to include five children (now four with the loss of my husband's beloved son, James), four in-laws, and a dozen grandchildren (plus three whose father married into the fold). Every member of our family, who might seem "average" to you, are truly amazing to their father/ grandfather and me.

I've been an employee and an employer. My husband and I have worked in our shared businesses, first, side by side, and in our recent entrepreneurial iterations, more independently. We've earned impressive financial success and have enjoyed having, and sharing, the prosperity our labors have provided. We've overcome adversity, battled hardships, and pressed on.

Like many of you reading these words, in addition to my writing avocation, I have a "real job" at which I labor daily. But what I've done, or haven't done, isn't the point of this book. My successes, as I define them, are simply a testament to the truth that if I can succeed, anyone can.

I fervently hope, and would like to believe, that there's value for you (and for your family, your team if you have one, and your community) in hearing how "an everyday person" did it. There's nothing particularly outstanding about me, other than my drive, determination, and persistence. I'm likely neither the smartest nor the most highly educated person in the room, but I will surely be among the most willing, disciplined, and responsible. I've worked hard to overcome self-doubt, defeat every obstacle, share my experiences, record my insights, and tell my story. I've soldiered on in all that I've done, including authoring this book, as you must do in your own quest for success.

In the end, this book isn't as much about my journey as it is about you. It's about your hopes and dreams—your attitudes and aspirations— your behaviors and beliefs. This is your guide to achieving success on your own terms and by your own definition. I hope the Simple Strategies message resonates with you, and that because of it, you decide to think differently and do things differently. My dream is that you'll put these Simple Success Strategies into practice, and that this book, and the work you'll do as a result of reading it, will have value and meaning as you set out on your own journey toward successfully living the life you've imagined.

If you want to share your success journey with me, or have questions to ask or observations to share along the way, please reach out to me at delores@delorescrum.com. You'll find my regular blog posts on success and other topics on that site as well, along with insights and observations regarding the ongoing success journey. I'll also keep you posted on future book projects and invite you to join the "Success Strategy Circle" of readers and friends. I hope you'll visit and enjoy being a part of the Simple Strategies community.

It's said a book is a gift to the world. If you feel moved to offer an expression of appreciation to me, or to the many authors who strive to contribute to our reader's entertainment, or their edification, please do so by writing and submitting a sincere review.

Eleanor Roosevelt said, "The future belongs to those who believe in the beauty of their dreams." Clarity in envisioning what you want and an unshakeable belief that you're worthy of attaining the life you've imagined are the first steps to attaining the success you deserve. Let's get started.

Foreword

"The more that you read, the more things you will know.
The more that you learn, the more places you'll go."
– Dr. Seuss

"Books are the plane, and the train, and the road. They are
the destination, and the journey. They are home."
– Anna Quindlen

"The book you don't read won't help."
– Jim Rohn

Why This Book?

THERE ARE HUNDREDS of different reasons people write and read books. Novelists write books that entertain. We read them because a well-told story is the purest, most enjoyable form of escapist entertainment. Academics pen works that educate and inform, and we read them to gain knowledge and understanding. Politicians seek to influence and persuade or enlighten others through their writings. We read their books to gain insight and understanding.

Books by business owners document approaches and practices that have contributed to their career success. We read them to help improve our company's performance or to advance in our chosen field. Biographical works may tell the stories of heroes and heroines and impart their acts of courage and valor. Some biographies relate the details of the protagonist's life, framing a rags-to-riches story and enthralling us with tales of worldwide fame gained and fabulous fortunes made. We read these works in the hope and belief that some secret within their pages may enable us to achieve those same lofty heights.

"Self-help" books, as this and related works are known, have a different set of objectives. They're often written to offer readers the strategies and practices that have proven valuable in an author's own experience or through observing the lives of others. The hope is that a reader's financial circumstances, relationships, health, or happiness—even all of the above—may improve as a result. Books in this genre are written and read by those who believe that words have power: power to encourage and enlighten, to move and inspire, to help and to guide. They're written by those who share the conviction that written words, translated into success-compatible attitudes, actions, and behaviors, practiced consistently by the reader, can create positive and lasting change.

This book is written with one goal—to help those committed to living more successfully and joyfully achieve the successful life they've imagined. The Seven Simple Success Strategies presented in the pages that follow have helped me and my family meet our business objectives and reach our financial goals. I'm living—we're living—life abundantly. Applying the PPPEEEZ strategies has enriched my personal life and blessed our family members' lives. Internalize the strategies we'll explore here together, make them an integral part of who you are and what you do every day, and live the abundant life you deserve.

Chapter **1**

Laying the Foundation

"The foundation stones for a balanced success are honesty, character, integrity, faith, love and loyalty."
– Zig Ziglar.

"A successful man is one who can lay a firm foundation with the bricks others have thrown at him."
– David Brinkley

"Great persons are great because of good, strong foundations on which they were able to build a character."
– Alfred Armand Montapert

The PPPEEEZ Strategy

"A vision without a strategy remains an illusion."
– Lee Bolman

POSITIVITY, PERSISTENCE, PRINCIPLES, Energy, Expertise, Emotion, and Zeal—these seven words present a smart and simple strategy for reaching and retaining a higher level of financial success and personal satisfaction. Logan Pearsall Smith, an American-born British essayist and critic (1865-1946) said "There are two things to aim at in life: first, to get what you want; and, after that, to enjoy it. Only the wisest of mankind achieve the second." The seven strategies presented here are designed to help you get what you want from life, and to ensure that getting what you want brings you joy and fulfillment.

Why PPPEEEZ? PPPEEEZ is an initialization inspired by the PEZ candy company. PEZ has a long and interesting history. PEZ says this in its North American Web Site (pez.com) About Us page. "An integral part of the American scene for approximately 50 years, PEZ Candy has been enjoyed by generations of Americans. Today, over 3 billion PEZ Candies are consumed annually in the USA alone. Available around the world in more than 80 countries, PEZ Candy and Dispensers truly have universal appeal." To me, that's a pretty impressive pedigree.

The letters in the PPPEEEZ strategy are easy to remember—three P'S, three E'S, and a Z. It's my hope that, if you hold fast to the Simple PPPEEEZ Strategies and internalize the message of this book, you will think of, and be inspired by, the PPPEEEZ success formula whenever, and wherever, you see a ubiquitous PEZ dispenser.

Like PEZ candy, the PPPEEEZ Simple Strategies for Successful Living are simple, and in my view, timeless. PEZ containers have evolved over the years, to reflect pop-culture icons and capitalize on the appeal of contemporary trends in children's entertainment, yet the candy inside remains essentially the same. The context in which the PPPEEEZ strategies are applied will evolve over time as well. The only constant in our world is change—change at an ever-accelerating pace and with an even more profound impact on our daily lives. But I cannot foresee a time when Positivity, Persistence, Principles, Energy, Expertise, Emotion, and Zeal are not a relevant and firm foundation for building a successful and happy life.

Strategies Move Mountains

"Strategy is a fancy word for coming up with a long-term plan and putting it into action."
– Ellie Pidot

"Success is 20% skills and 80% strategy. You might know how to succeed, but more importantly, what's your plan to succeed?"
– Jim Rohn

WHY STRATEGIES? WHY not suggestions or tactics, blueprints or plans? Wikipedia suggests that "a strategy is a high-level plan to achieve one or more goals under conditions of uncertainty." It goes on to say that "strategy generally involves setting goals, determining actions to achieve the goals, and mobilizing resources to execute the actions. A strategy describes how the ends (goals) will be achieved by the means (resources) available." Merriam-Webster's online dictionary defines strategy as "a careful plan or method for achieving a particular goal, usually over a long period of time."

In his 2009 book The Global Emerging Market – Strategic Management and Economics, Vladimir Kvint says that strategy is, "a system of finding, formulating, and developing a doctrine that will ensure long-term success if followed faithfully." That's our aim here—to present, for your consideration and internalization, a surefire success formula. To be sure, you'll encounter obstacles along your success journey. Some will be mere bumps in the road. Others may be, or seem to be, massive sink holes. But you'll strategize, act, reflect on your success (or lack thereof), and keep trying. You'll keep on keeping on because that's what success strategists do.

Imagine, for example, you're tasked with moving a small mountain. The mountain in this scenario resulted from a landslide, and now the only road into or out of your community is blocked by several cubic tons of rock and earth. You're the mayor of your town, and everyone is looking to you for a solution.

What will you need to move that mountain? What resources do you have at your disposal? Will you approach the mountain with picks and shovels or bring in earth-moving equipment that will make the job easier and faster? Do you need outside expertise, or do you and your townspeople have the know-how it takes to succeed in this mountain-moving endeavor? Will your community rally around your plan and support your suggestions, or criticize you for pursing a course of action that may be too complicated and costly? Moving that mountain will require a simple, successful strategy!

Like moving a mountain, overcoming obstacles that block our path to successful living, or impede our enjoyment of the good life we and our families deserve, requires successful strategies. We must rid ourselves of unwanted thoughts, attitudes, and actions that hinder our progress. We must embrace progressive, proven-effective strategies that will "ensure long-term success if followed faithfully." The objective of this book is to explore seven strategies that have worked for me and that have been validated by others' success journeys as well. These proven strategies will work for you, too, if you're willing to invest the time and effort that achieving and maintaining a successful life, in every context, requires.

Simple Isn't Easy

> "Success is simple, but isn't easy because it demands execution, not intentions."
> – Orrin Woodward

THERE'S NOTHING DIFFICULT or complex in the PPPEEEZ formula. It's understandable and straightforward, simple to grasp and easy to comprehend. It's direct and instructive—no hidden messages or deeper meanings. The strategies that unfold in the following pages are basic and uncomplicated.

But applying PPPEEEZ strategies to everyday living isn't easy. Tom Hanks played the role of an all-woman's baseball team manager in the 1992 movie "A League of Their Own". His character, Jimmy Dugan, said this to encourage his team: "If it wasn't hard, everyone would do it. It's the hard that makes it great." Living a successful life, achieving what you want, and enjoying it, isn't easy either. If it wasn't hard to do, everyone would be happy, wealthy, healthy, and fit. We'd all be successful by our own definition.

Few of us are born into wealth and prosperity. Fewer still will hit the Power Ball lottery or play a Mega-Millions slot machine that serendipitously lands on red, white, and blue triple sevens. Most of us will have to work, some of us harder than others, for what we acquire. We'll have to build a business or a career from the ground up. Carving out "the good life" of our dreams will require making sound choices every day. We'll have to give up some things and embrace others. We'll likely need to change our thinking and alter our habits. And none of it will be easy. Like losing weight or saving for college or building a retirement nest egg, the "thinking" behind successful living is easy . . . it's the "doing" that's difficult.

Reading this book will not make it one bit easier to live successfully. But consistently applying the PPPEEEZ strategies to the choices you make and the actions you take can make a difference. You can improve your quality of life (and that of your family), advance in your career or profession, succeed in your business, and enjoy every day to the fullest . . . simply (but not easily) by choosing, consciously and deliberately, to live successfully.

Actions Speak Louder Than Words

"Well done is better than well said."
– Benjamin Franklin

YOU AND I know people, personally or by reputation and observation, whose words speak louder than their actions. Wiktionary provides a collection of idiomatic phrases, including: "all hat and no cattle"; "all talk and no show"; "all show and no go"; "all sizzle and no steak"; and "all wick and no candle" to describe people who are "full of big talk but lacking action, power or substance" . . . in a word, "pretentious." As one of my teammates in our business is fond of saying, in a twist on the adage that "an ounce of prevention is worth a pound of cure", "An ounce of pretention is worth a pound of manure."

Living successfully requires ACTION, and ACTIONS Speak Louder than Words. We can talk all we want about what we should do, what we might do, and what we ought to do. In Texas, you might even prattle on and on about what you're "fixin" to do. But a lifetime of talking about what we want to have, and who we want to be, won't move any of us one whit closer to becoming our best and most successful self. To pass the test, you have to study. To be a hitter, you have to spend time in the batting cage. To get that promotion, you have to measure up. To move up, you have to step up. To succeed, you must take action.

Sinking free throws like Steve Nash, holder of the NBA's all-time leading free throw percentage, takes talent, sure . . . but more than talent, it takes practice. Racking up tennis championships like Serena Williams takes incredible athletic prowess . . . but more than that, it takes strategic action. It's said that it takes ten years to fully master a craft. Achieving mastery will require years, sometimes a lifetime, of determination and dedication. Whether your field is acting, music, business, law, accounting, teaching, or preaching, whatever you do in life that earns you a living, and upon which you will build your ideal future, takes action. Achieve is an action verb—and actions speak louder than words. The only place success comes before work, we're told, is in the dictionary.

Defining Success

"Define success on your own terms, achieve it by your own rules, and build a life you're proud to live."
– Anne Sweeney

IT'S YOUR LIFE! Only you can define what "success" looks like to you. Your success vision may include a specific net worth, a townhome in the city, and a weekend place somewhere on the water. A fancy car, a closet full of designer threads, and a safe full of jewelry may be important to you. Or none of these tangible possessions may be germane to your success vision.

Perhaps your definition of success includes a close and loving family and a collection of interesting and supportive friends. Creating a college fund for your children, or completing a home remodel that updates your living space and increases your comfort may resonate with you. A working environment where your contribution is appreciated, where you can grow and thrive, where you have free time to enjoy the life you've crafted may be more important to you than ever-upward mobility or business ownership. So long as your financial needs are met, and you can both support your family and save for retirement, you may not long for more and your dreams may be fulfilled.

Unless you're going it alone, it's important that you and your spouse or life partner agree on a success vision. You will likely find that divergent visions of success make achieving a happy life very, very difficult. Couples with one partner who wants and needs to be in the top 1 or 3 or 5 percent (in net worth or household income or both) to feel successful, paired with an 'other' who is totally content with middle- or upper-middle-class "status", may always be at odds. If one partner wants children and believes every child should have a pet or two, and the other prefers the role of aunt or uncle to being a mom or dad and is allergic to pet dander, it may be difficult to achieve a happy, successful life. And while domestic peace and harmony may not be essential to success as you define it, it's hard to argue that a happy home life is not generally regarded as part and parcel of success.

According to a 2017 Pew report, almost half (42 percent) of American adults did not live with a spouse or partner. You may find the complete online article, entitled "8 facts about love and marriage in America" (https://www.pewresearch.org/fact-tank/2019/02/13/8-facts-about-love-and-marriage/) interesting reading. If you've presently chosen to neither marry nor to be part of a long-term monogamous relationship, you'll be able to define success on your own terms. You'll be "exempt" from the requirement of compromise as a prerequisite for peaceful coexistence. The expectations and achievements of others, including parents or siblings, may impact your thinking, but your success vision can be unilateral and uncompromising. Nevertheless, you'll probably have a set point that reflects, to some degree, society's success definition.

Google "How Do Most Americans Define Success?". You'll find an array of responses to the "What is success? "question. An October, 2019 article entitled "Americans have a nuanced definition of success—but think everyone else only cares about money", is a good starting point in arriving at your own success definition. This article, by Jessica Klein, reports that "A new study" (5,242 subjects) "finds that, while most people in the U. S. still think society cares more about money and status, they're wrong. Most people personally value relationships and character more." (https://www.fastcompany.com/90411846), Klein continues, "Public perception of success in the U. S is totally misguided. While 92% of people believe others care most about fame and fortune, fewer than 10% factor those qualities into their own success. Most of those surveyed", she adds, "believe everyone else around them wants money, status, and power, while what they personally want is strong relationships, a better character, and to be a part of a community." Interesting. Does this information have meaning for you?

An October 2, 2019 Gallup posting, "Americans' Perceptions of Success in the U. S." (RJ Reinhart and Zacc Ritter) reports similar findings. "A new report by Populace and Gallup finds that while less than 10% of Americans personally define success in status-oriented, comparative, or zero-sum ways, they largely believe other Americans do. The report also finds that there is a disconnect between American's perceptions of their attainment of personal success and what they believe society views as success." Thought-provoking. Are these findings consistent with your success perspective?

The Populace and Gallup report continues "Many more Americans are achieving success according to their own views . . . than what they believe to be society's views". Further, the study's assertion that "those with a lower household income report lower success attainment scores" isn't surprising, but that the relationship between income and success self-rankings "flattens once household income reaches $75,000 to $99,000" may be a less expected result. The article is worth reading in its entirety.

In a January 27, 2018 article by Shawn Langlois (www.market-watch.com/story/this-is-what-success-looks-like-to-the-average-amer-ican-2018-01-22) the author reports data from a ThermoSoft poll of 2,000 people. "Interestingly", the article states, "77% (of the respondents) said they wouldn't want more than $1 million in annual income, even if it was offered." This reading offers a success vision that includes a target home value ($461,000), freedom, work/life balance and working from home.

Finally, as food for thought as we approach the work ahead at the end of this chapter, I offer you "How Do You Define Success? How You Do Impacts You In a Big Way, Gallup Poll Says." Steve Farber, Founder, The Extreme Leadership Institute, advises that "Fame and fortune may or may not define success for you, but you owe it to yourself to make sure one way or another. So", Farber asked his readers, "do you think you have to be well known and rich to have a successful life? Luckily", he observed, "that's not what most people's true, inner hearts care about—and that is what really matters."

Flash back to the last decade, and the "What is Success?" responses are strikingly similar. A Business Insider article posted by Jacquelyn Smith on October, 2014, and the research that supports Smith's writing, suggests that there is no "one size fits all" success definition. A 2011 survey from Strayer University found that "a whopping 90% of survey respondents" (2011 Americans ages eighteen and up) "believe that success is more about happiness than power, possessions, or prestige."

Quoting from Strayer's article, "[These results] indicate a clear change in the way Americans are thinking about their personal journey," says Dr. Michael Plater, president of Strayer University. "It's no longer about the car or the house. Instead, people are focused on leading a fulfilling life, whether that means finding a better career, achieving personal goals, or spending more time with their families. Sixty-seven percent of surveyed Americans associate success with achieving personal goals; 66% cited good relationships with friends and family; and 60% said loving what you do for a living. "It's challenging to quantify and pinpoint what defines success," Plater continues, "since every individual has his or her own unique view and personal experience."

In his 2008 book Flight Plan: How to Achieve More, Faster Than You Ever Dreamed Possible, Brian Tracy asserts that "your first and greatest responsibility to yourself is to become absolutely clear about what it is that you really want." He continues, "Virtually all of us have four main goals in common. These are (1) to be fit, be healthy and live a long life; (2) to do work we enjoy and be well paid for it; (3) to be in happy relationships with people we love and respect and who love and respect us in return; and (4) to achieve financial independence so we never have to worry about money again." These goals, as well as others woven throughout this book, are timeless.

Success, then, would appear to have these essential four components. In my world, a balanced success strategy would start with "Financial Wellbeing". I believe that financial peace of mind is paramount to thriving and surviving—to success itself. Granted, "financial wellbeing" is relative, and you and I, you and your family, you and your colleagues, you and your friends and acquaintances, will all have divergent opinions about what this term entails. But without a sense of financial security there is stress, there is worry, there is insecurity. As I see it, absent sound fiscal footing, there's no path to successfully living the life you deserve.

Productive work in a positive, supportive environment is a second essential success component. Later chapters of this book address this success element more fully, but no success vision is complete without a joyful way to earn an adequate living.

Enjoying positive family relationships—Cultivating a circle of interesting and supportive friends—Having a sense of connection . . . our life-experiences tell us, and the readings in this chapter confirm, relationships are part and parcel of the success package. You'll benefit from articulating both your vision and your investment strategy for relating to the people in your life who matter.

Finally, for most of us, health is not a matter of chance, but of choice. The degree of health we enjoy is directly dependent on whether or not we consciously and consistently manage our health habits. What we eat, and how much—what we drink, and how much as well— the exercise we get – the medications or supplements we take. We'll explore these matters more deeply throughout our later pages, but for now, it's time to start devising a concrete health plan and to adopt healthy living practices as an important contributor to success.

The balance of this chapter presents a framework designed to help you crystallize your current success vision and articulate your present-day success definition. Blank spaces are included in the following pages so that you can place a written record of your thoughts here. If you chose to share this book with others and wish to keep your responses private, or if the space provided is too small or you find the format awkward, simply request a PDF of this and all Simple Strategies worksheets (delores@delorescrum.com), and you'll receive them via a follow-up email. If this framework somehow doesn't work for you, change it. If the terms used don't resonate with you, substitute your own vocabulary or vernacular.

Within this book, or separate and apart from it, I urge and encourage you to draft a written Successful Living Strategy that includes YOUR definition of key terms, considers and records what is and isn't important to you, and reflects a set of "SMART" (Specific, Measurable, Attainable, Relevant, and Time-Bound) Goals, along with specific, written objectives for attaining them. Do yourself (and your family) a favor. Embrace the challenge and opportunity to create your written success vision and craft your success definition. There's no time like the present and nothing to be gained by waiting!

Success Strategy Guide for Articulating Your Success Vision, Goals, and Strategies

1. If these parameters are important to you, you may wish to establish a minimum annual income level (e.g. To achieve financial success by my definition, I must earn no less than $ _____ annually) and or a cumulative net worth goal (e.g. To consider myself financially successful, I must have a net worth of no less than $ _____ by age _____.)

2. If discretionary income and a "spending allowance" are important to you, you may want to complete the following statement: "To enjoy financial success by my definition, I must have no less than $ _____ in disposable monthly income (funds available to spend as I choose after all of my bills have been paid and my creditors satisfied)."

3. Certain trappings traditionally associated with North American society's success definition may or may not be important to you. If they are, you may choose to explore your goals in that regard. "Achieving financial success by my definition means that I ". . . (Here are some examples of things or circumstances that might matter to you: owning (vs. renting) your home; establishing and maintaining a savings threshold to protect against accident, injury, or loss of employment; protecting your credit score and ensuring your borrowing power; reducing your debt to more than 10% of your annual earnings, etc.).

Note: If North American society isn't the milieu in which you operate, adapt this summary of "things" that matter to you and your plans for obtaining them to your situation.

4. To consider myself fiscally responsible and to ensure that I provide for my future needs (so that I can retain financial independence throughout my lifetime), I will adopt the following specific savings and or investment strategies (e.g. contributing to my company's 401K program, opening an IRA account and making annual IRA contributions, setting aside a percentage of monthly income, etc.).

Note: Likewise, here. If your environment doesn't fit this North American norm, how will you plan ahead and provide for your future?

5. I have other financial goals, wants, and needs to consider myself financially fit and monetarily healthy. Those goals for obtaining and sustaining monetary health and my specific strategies for assuring that I meet them are described here.

6. My success definition includes a healthy work environment. I define a work setting in which I can achieve my definition of success and enjoy the work I do as including (for example: the ability to work independently or with minimum supervision; working closely with people I enjoy and respect; being rewarded for my efforts with increased responsibility; having the opportunity for advancement and the potential for increased compensation.) My healthy work environment definition is summarized here, along with the specific strategies that will help me achieve my work environment goals.

7. Success in relationships, by my definition, means the following: (for example: finding a primary life partner; having close ties to parents, siblings or extended family; enjoying close friends or confidants; relating to a network of friends and acquaintances, participating in an organized religion or joining a club or philanthropic group). Ensuring that my relationships with others contribute to my sense of joy and of living successfully involves these strategies.

8. I define success in terms of my physical health and sense of personal well-being in the following ways: (e.g. you may wish to record an ideal weight, a weekly exercise or physical activity goal, a commitment to "healthy eating," etc.). Achieving my self-care and or health care goals requires these specific actions (which might involve both doing the "right" things to support your definition of health and "not" doing the things that are potentially harmful or detrimental).

9. Ralph Waldo Emerson said this: "That (man) is a success who has lived well, laughed often and loved much; Who has gained the respect of intelligent (men) and the love of children; who has filled (his) niche and accomplished (his) task; Who leaves the world better than (he) found it, whether by an improved poppy or a perfect poem or a rescued soul; Who never lacked appreciation of earth's beauty or failed to express it; Who looked for the best in others and gave the best (he) had." These 5-7 sentences summarize my current success vision and definition.

Additional Successful Living Strategies for Couples

IN ANY LIST of factors contributing to family stress or unresolved family issues, money almost always comes first. Disagreements about saving and spending, or about time and energy invested in work vs. quality time spent with the family plague many contemporary relationships. Disparate views about successful living often lead to arguments, hurt feelings, and resentment. Conflicts regarding money—or the lack thereof—can sabotage relationships and rob couples of joy and fulfillment. In the extreme, controversy surrounding finances is generally accepted as a leading cause of divorce.

If you're in a committed relationship that involves the sharing of financial and other resources, chances are you and your significant other don't always see eye-to-eye. Talking through your individual responses to the first 5 individual success strategies may help. If reaching financial harmony, as a couple, is important to you, the following exercise might be a good starting point.

1. In the area of finances, we agree that . . .

2. Financially speaking, the following individual financial views are a source of controversy in our relationship.

3. As a couple, we can take the following specific steps to achieve greater financial harmony.

Related Reading

https://www.cnbc.com/2015/02/04/money-is-the-leading-cause-of-stress-in-relationships.html

https://www.forbes.com/sites/jenniferbarrett/2018/01/17/why-we-fight-over-money-so-much-and-how-to-stop/#26eb6d0b12b4

4. As a couple, we can support one another's individual work success and enjoyment in the following specific ways.

5. Here are some steps we can take to improve our interactions and gain greater enjoyment from our relationships with family and friends.

6. We have identified the following ways to contribute to one another's health and physical well-being.

7. These 3-5 sentences express our family's success vision and definition.

Chapter Notes:

1. *There are a number of resources, some available at little or no cost, that can contribute to improved financial health. Credit counselling, debt consolidation, and other steps have proven successful for some individuals and or couples who avail themselves of outside assistance.*

2. *This chapter did not address achieving family harmony in every aspect of life, but rather focused on the big three—finances (and work), relationships, and health. There are many other areas of family life that contribute to or detract from our feelings of success and enjoyment of life. Some examples include the desire to have or not to have children; the ways in which children will be disciplined, educated, and "entertained"; the presence or absence of pets in the home; the importance of monogamy in the relationship; the tolerance for tobacco, alcohol, or recreational drug use—and so much more. Once again, any aspect of life that adversely impacts either the success achieved or the joy experienced may require greater focus, frank and open discussion, and positive attitudinal or behavioral change.*

3. *If progress cannot be made or desired results achieved, outside assistance in addressing these or other family "problems" may be needed. In some relationships, formal couples or family counseling can help. Getting the successful life you deserve in every context, when you're part of a couple, requires not only commitment, but often necessitates compromise. Getting your way is often far less satisfying than reaching agreement on, and then working toward the "Optimum Way." Identify and strive for Win-Win opportunities and solutions in this and every context.*

Chapter 2

The First "P" = Positivity

> "It's most important that you surround yourself with positivity always, and have it in your mind at all times."
> – Tyler Perry

> "Optimism is the most important human trait, because it allows us to evolve our ideas, to improve our situation, and to hope for a better tomorrow."
> – Seth Godin

IF YOU REMEMBER nothing else from this book, remember this: Be Positive. In no time at all, you can find literally hundreds of online resources that will define positivity, help you understand positivity, aid you in measuring your level of positivity, and support you in increasing your positivity. With the internet as your guide, you can identify, download and utilize positivity resources, and learn what it means to be, and discover more about how to be, positive. You can explore the impact that positivity can have, not only on the quality of your life, but the lives of those you love. Positivity impacts your success in the workplace and affects, for good or for bad, those with whom you cross paths, whether frequently, or simply from time to time.

It's not what you know about positivity that matters – it's what you do with what you know. Knowledge has no inherent power to help us achieve our hopes, live our dreams, and accomplish our goals. We cannot gain the benefits of what we've discovered, in this or any context, either through insight or experience, until what we "should" do shapes our thoughts and guides our actions. To gain the benefits that positivity affords, to take the first step on the road to successful living, we must Be Positive!

Attitude Isn't Everything, It's the Only Thing!

"An attitude of positive expectation is the mark
of a superior personality."
– Brian Tracy

"A positive attitude awakens inner strength,
energy, motivation, and initiative."
– Ramez Sasson

YOU'VE HEARD THE words, read a quote, or seen a poster that says "Your attitude determines your altitude". Thomas Jefferson said: "Nothing can stop the man with right mental attitude from achieving his goal; nothing on earth can help the man with the wrong mental attitude." So, what is "right" and what is "wrong" from an attitudinal standpoint? And how does our attitude contribute to living a successful life?

Each year, our work team participates in a team retreat. Part of our advance retreat preparation involves reading a retreat text that becomes a lesson topic when we meet to look at the year ahead. One year, our retreat was based on what is, in my view, one of the most impactful books I've ever read, and that you will ever read. The Happiness Advantage by Shawn Achor, subtitled The Seven Principles of Positive Psychology That Fuel Success and Performance at Work, provides a schematic for positivity. More than that, Achor's happiness principles are well researched and scientifically grounded.

Here's what the book jacket promises: "[Achor] shows us how to capitalize on the Happiness Advantage to improve our performance and maximize our potential. Conventional wisdom holds that if we work hard, we will be more successful, and if we are more successful, then we'll be happy. If we can just find that great job, win that next promotion, lose those five pounds, happiness will follow. But recent discoveries in the field of positive psychology have shown that this formula is actually backward: Happiness fuels success, not the other way around. When we are positive, our brains become more engaged, creative, motivated, energetic, resilient, and productive at work." For a synopsis of Achor's Seven Principles, watch the 2013 TED talk "The Happy Secret to Better Work."

The right attitude is simple to define. The right attitude is a positive attitude—an outlook that holds a positive world view. Positivists believe that the past is prologue, the present is pleasant, and the future is promising. Those with a positive attitude trust both themselves and others to do the right thing. Positive thinking tells us that what the mind can conceive can be achieved—that the only time we fail is the last time we try—that "whether we think we can, or think we cannot, either way— we're right" (Henry Ford).

Positivity is rich with possibilities and short on excuses. Positivity is rife with potential and scarce on apology. Positivity isn't woulda, coulda, shoulda . . . it's I Did! I did what I said I would, accomplished what I knew I could, and am living the life I know I should. Positivity enriches our own life and enhances the lives of those we love. If there is a panacea, a cure for what ails us and a way to make all right with the world, it's positive thinking and positive living.

While the right attitude is simple to define, it's not easy to achieve and sometimes difficult to maintain. My take on the right attitude is inspired by Rudyard Kipling's IF: A Father's Advice to His Son. "If you can keep a smile upon you when all around you would have you wear a frown; If you can keep your head up high with purpose, when all around you try to bring you down; If you accept that, just like steel, you're hardened, that trials and tribulations pass in time; If you are ever grateful for good fortune, and willing to share all it is you've gained—Yours is the Earth and Everything that's in it, And—which is more—you will know what others think is secret—"happiness" (and the life you deserve) "will be what you have found."

Make up your mind to be happy. Embrace positivity. Wake up every day, and make a conscious choice that, no matter how the day unfolds, your attitude will start and remain positive. Keep a happiness journal (you can actually purchase these online!). Each day, record three gratitudes. Focus on the good that came your way—the encouraging words from a colleague, the hug from a child, support from your partner, unconditional acceptance from your parent, the goal you met, the recognition you received, the obstacle you overcame.

Don't wait for a new month or a new year. There's nothing to be gained by waiting. NOW is the time to get started on your journey toward a more positive, more successful, more joyful you. Seize this moment, own this day!

Pessimism Is Poison

"If I continually focus on what I don't have, my life
will always be completely empty despite the fact that
it's completely full."
– Craig D. Lounsbrough

"The pessimist may call the optimist a fool; but who is
more foolish, the happy individual who expects more
happiness or the one who fills his life with bitterness and
has only more dispair to look forward to?"
– Wayne Gerard Trotman

THE WORLD WAS stunned when, on November 18th, 1978, 909 inhabitants (304 of them children) of Jonestown, the Guyana settlement founded by Jim Jones, leader of the People's Temple, died of "apparent cyanide poisoning." Wikipedia cites this incident as "the greatest single loss of American civilian lives in a deliberate act until the terrorist attacks of September 11, 2001." The citizens of Jonestown committed mass suicide by willingly drinking cyanide-laced grape-flavored liquid. The phrase "drinking the Kool-Aid" arose from this incident, and in popular use has come to mean "knowingly going along with a doomed or dangerous idea because of peer pressure."

I submit to you that pessimism is no less a doomed and dangerous idea, no less a threat to successful living than "drinking the Kool-Aid" was on that fateful day. No, it might not result in bodily harm or cause immediate death, but pessimism wounds (sometimes mortally) our spirit, destroys our dreams, and saps our strength. Holding a pessimistic life view obviates, obliterates, and utterly decimates the joy that we could have, the optimism that we should have, and ultimately, taken to the extreme, the love that we might have.

What's really wrong with the world today? What stands between us and the successful life we deserve? What robs us of sleep, steals our peace of mind, raises our blood pressure, piles on the pounds, and sends us to an early grave . . . pessimism. Don't take my word for it! Simply conduct an online search for "the effects of pessimism" and read for yourself.

Watch or listen to the evening news, and what's the gist? The negativists, sensationalists, and pessimists would have us believe we're in grave danger—threats loom on the horizon—government can't be trusted—people, generally, are no good. Listen to the cynics and naysayers, and you'll soon believe that "those" who haven't gotten us already are out to get us for sure. If you take the bad news to heart, you'll fear that not only is the world a dangerous place, but we're not even safe in our own homes. Hackers are out to steal our identity. A thief may be stalking the neighborhood or lurking right outside the door. People are assaulted, even killed, in broad daylight. Law enforcement officers are corruptible and may not offer equal protection to all.

I'm not saying everything we fear couldn't happen, I'm just saying it probably won't happen. I'm not saying that some people don't behave badly. Sadly, and tragically, especially in recent years, a few people have wreaked havoc on our streets, in our schools and even within our churches. But, and it's a really "big but," neither fear nor anxiety will make us one whit safer. The worry, anxiety, and stress we feel because bad things might happen makes us sick, tired, irritable, unproductive, and old before our time. Our challenge, yours and mine, is remaining positive in a dangerously pessimistic society. Don't buy into "their" negativity and paranoia—don't drink the Kool-Aid!

Google "the negative effects of pessimism." I stopped counting after 30 results pages. Here are just a few quick highlights: "5 Reasons Why Being a Pessimist Can Have a Negative Impact on Your Life" (magforliving.com); "Pessimism Can Hurt Your Heart" (WebMD); "The Negative Effects of Pessimism" (energize.com); "Are You a Negaholic?" "5 Ways Pessimism is Ruining Your Life" (michaelhyatt.com). In fairness, you'll find a few contrarian articles, but overwhelmingly, behavioral scientists and medical practitioners laud the positive effects of optimism, praise positivity, and warn against the deleterious effects of a negative mindset.

Here are a few simple steps toward maintaining a positive, optimistic attitude. Stop watching television news, reading the headlines, and listening to talk radio. Apart from keeping generally informed about what's happening here at home and around the world, do you really need to know how bad things are (or are purported to be)? The constant bombardment of negative, threatening messages simply cannot be healthy for our psyches!

Tune in to your favorite newscast if you must; just mute any story that sensationalizes violence or "glorifies" the perpetrator. Keep your newspaper subscription; simply skip any story that focuses on the bad actor rather than the unfortunate victims. Tune your radio to a station that makes you smile, whatever genre that might be. Just change the dial if you come across a message that's upsetting or incendiary. Whatever the media or message, if it doesn't contribute to your positivity, and instead stokes your negativity, ditch it.

I'm a lot happier without the constant barrage of broadcast pessimism and press negativity. The Life and Arts section of our local newspaper keeps me informed on how to enjoy my community and contains puzzles (Jumble, Crosswords, and Word Challenges) that keep my brain active and engaged. Pessimism has no place in my line of endeavor, and probably is out of place in your field as well. In our business as party and event rental professionals, our primary objective is helping people celebrate and enjoy life. How can we do that if we're anxious and fearful? How can you be happy and joyful if you're worried and apprehensive?

While pessimism has no place in my life or yours, realism and practicality are positive attributes. Making light of real personal, professional, financial, or other day-to-day threats may lead to disaster. If you worked for Enron, perhaps you could have sensed the toxic atmosphere, foreseen the cataclysm, and acted accordingly. If you invested with Madoff, you might have done well to heed those "too-good-to-be-true" warnings. Failing to plan and prepare for contingencies that present a very real threat to our well-being isn't prudent. Ignoring the evacuation warnings and coming face-to-face with hurricane Katrina, Harvey, Maria, or Florence, may not be the wisest course of action.

I agree with the adage that "worry is the advance price we pay for troubles that may never come." At the same time, ignoring the risks and realities of living in our time can be dangerous and irresponsible. Strive to achieve a healthy balance between positivity and practicality.

Let Your Light Shine

"When you are joyful, when you say yes to life
and have fun and project positivity all around you,
you become a sun in the center of every constellation,
and people want to be near you."
– Shannon L. Alder

"Positive thinking is more than just a tagline.
It changes the way we behave. And I firmly believe
that when I am positive, it not only makes me better,
but it also makes those around me better."
– Harvey Mackay

IF YOU'RE GOING to be positive anyway, why not be a beacon of positivity for others? Here are a few suggestions for letting your light shine.

Start each day with hope—end each day with gratitude. Somewhere in the middle, find a few moments of quiet time for reflection. Appreciate the beauty around and within you. Read Desiderata. The text of this 1927 poem by Max Ehrmann is easily accessible online. Study scripture or writings from your religion of choice . . . or broaden your horizons, and perhaps your tolerance, by reading from someone else's book. Meditate with music or find solace in silence. Do whatever it takes to put yourself in a positive frame of mind. Keep a Happiness Record and a Gratitude Journal. Focus on the good, and let go of the bad.

In my experience, unless you have boundless time and energy and a really high tolerance for disappointment and frustration, there's likely little to be gained from attempting to convert a pessimist. You can try, certainly. Leave them cheerful notes. Gift them with The Hundred Simple Secrets of Happy People (David Niven, PhD) or Shawn Achor's The Happiness Advantage (previously referenced). Perhaps, when they see all the benefits you're deriving from positivity, they'll even ask for your secret. "Have you lost weight?" "Did you have some work done?" "Is that a new hairstyle [or suit, or whatever]?" Positivity sparkles and shines.

If your light doesn't illuminate the negativists in your circle, distance yourself from the whiners and complainers. Avoid the "bitchers" and the moaners. Friends and associates who aren't lifting you up are pulling you down. Disassociate yourself from the back-stabbers and backbiters. Surround yourself with like-minded individuals. Keep company with those who are long on compliments and short on criticism—those who give credit where credit is due and shoulder their share of the blame when things go wrong.

Join groups that do good things. Get involved as a volunteer or donor. Select a cause or causes, and let those you choose to support know they can count on you. Serve on the Board or join a committee for a non-profit organization whose mission inspires you. You'll reap an abundance of blessings, including the opportunity to meet committed, passionate people who put their resources (of time and money) where their mouths are. Hearing those you've helped, in whatever small measure, describe the positive impact your group or organization has had on their lives and their families is its own reward. Encourage others to get involved as well, and multiply the good that you do. Doing "good" feels good and is a sure cure for poisonous pessimism.

Take some time now, or after you've finished reading this book, to develop your Personal Positivity Plan (PPP). You may find the following format helpful, and if not, create your own. But don't fail to make your PPP. Failing to plan is tantamount to planning to fail. Document a written PPP and start reaping the rewards of positivity today. Do it: for yourself, your family, your career or business, your friends and colleagues, your work team or play team(s). There's no time like the present and nothing to be gained by waiting.

Personal Positivity Success Strategies

1. Starting now, I will take the following daily actions to begin and end each and every day in a positive frame of mind.

2. Within the week, I will identify positive family members, friends, colleagues, and associates who can and will support my positivity commitment. My positive circle of family, friends, colleagues, and associates includes:

3. Within the month, I will identify pessimistic/negative family members, friends, colleagues, and associates, and will, when and where I can, limit my involvement with them. The negativists I will seek to avoid include:

4. No more than ninety days from today, I will have identified at least one group, club, or organization that interests me. I will demonstrate my support in the following ways (examples include volunteering time, donating goods or services, adopting a giving plan, etc.):

5. No more than six months from today, I will have raised my personal positivity quotient (the percentage of time when I feel positive, optimistic, and hopeful) no less than 10%. I will have read 10% Happier by Dan Harris. Here are my positivity plans for being 10% happier:

6. No more than nine months from today, I will be happier, more productive, and more successful in my work as a result of reading and applying Shawn Achor's The Happiness Advantage. My specific plan for achieving improved performance and increased success at work (including both what I will do and what I will refrain from doing) are documented here.

7. Over the next year, I will cultivate positivity enhancing actions, attitudes, and behaviors. Here are some specific actions that may help me achieve greater positivity:

8. Over the next year, I will avoid actions, attitudes, and behaviors that may allow negativity into my life. Here are some specific actions, attitudes, and behaviors I intend to avoid:

9. Each year, I will record 5-7 SMART Personal Positivity (PP) goals and set clear and compelling objectives that will ensure I remain positive, hopeful, and optimistic. My first PP Goals and Objectives are:

Chapter 3

The Second "P" = Persistence

"Nothing in this world can take the place of persistence.
Talent will not: nothing is more common
than unsuccessful men with talent.
Genius will not: unrewarded genius is almost a proverb.
Education will not:
the world is full of educated derelicts.
Persistence and determination alone are omnipotent."
– Calvin Coolidge

IF THERE ACTUALLY is a secret to success, that secret is Persistence. In Chapter 1, you, or you and your life partner, crafted a successful living definition. Chapter 2 helped you outline a Personal Positivity Plan. Nothing that came before this chapter and nothing that will follow is of any consequence whatsoever without the second "P," Persistence. As we know, successful living is simple—but not easy. And when the going gets tough, you'll always have two choices: give in and give up, or get going! Get your "go on" and get moving, or keep your "no on" and stay put. Shoot for the moon and know that, if you fall short, at least you'll land among the stars.

Perhaps you remember The Little Engine That Could. If you don't, find a copy and read it! Wikipedia provides fascinating insight into the story's origin and iterations. In 2007, the National Education Association included Platt & Munk's 1930 version of the story as one of its Teacher Top 100 Books for Children. Why? Because "the story is used to teach children the value of optimism" (otherwise known as positivity) "and hard work" (otherwise known as Persistence). The Little Engine that thought it could "do it" did. It wasn't easy to pull all those cars. Other bigger, stronger engines wouldn't even try. But the little blue engine didn't give up, though the hill was steep and the load was heavy. In the happy ending, that brave little train arrived at its destination – full of happiness and pride.

What will you do when faced with challenges and obstacles? How will you respond when the naysayers belittle you and your ideas? Where will you find the courage and fortitude to persist when the path of least resistance is right there in front of you? Hone your powers of persistence and you, too, can find that happy ending.

You Can Only Finish What You Start

"Starting is not most people's problem,
staying, continuing and finishing is."
– Darren Hardy

"So many fail because they don't get started — they don't go. They don't overcome inertia. They don't begin.
– W. Clement Stone

INERTIA MAY BE the single greatest obstacle to successful living. A body at rest tends to stay at rest . . . a body in motion tends to stay in motion. A person who hasn't initiated tends not to initiate . . . a person who has initiated tends to continue. So here you are, facing the ultimate question. Will you always do what you've always done and always get what you've always gotten? Or will you take the proverbial bull by the horns, seize the day, and capture the moment?

What, exactly, are you waiting for? Are you, like many people, "Waiting for the fish to bite or waiting for wind to fly a kite? Or waiting for Friday night or waiting perhaps for their Uncle Jake or a pot to boil or a better break or a string of pearls or a pair of pants or a wig with curls or another chance? Everyone is just waiting." (Dr. Seuss) As obvious as it sounds, you cannot finish what you do not start. Yet many of us start nothing. We're waiting for motivation. We're hoping for inspiration. But we're doing nothing. You can't finish what you don't start.

What would you do if you knew you couldn't fail? Well, the only time you fail is the last time you try, so get your "go" on. Ask Google for "best stories about overcoming adversity." You'll find ordinary people, people like you and me, who have accomplished extraordinary things under difficult and adverse circumstances. They prevailed, because they persevered. They got up and got going. Read Daymond John's Rise and Grind. The book jacket promises "Daymond reveals how we can all rise and grind our way to the success and fulfillment we seek. He shows how grit and persistence helped him overcome the obstacles he has faced in his own life, and ultimately fueled his success." 'Rise and Grind' not only presents Daymond John's own inspiring story, but offers valuable life lessons by the equally awe-inspiring men and women of vision and accomplishment profiled in his pages.

Successful people typically begin their journey with a dream or an idea or a vision. You've got dreams, ideas, and vision, too. Maybe you've conceived a way to improve your work processes or systems. Perhaps you've discovered a new way of doing something or something new to do. It's possible you're the one who will develop the next Facebook, Instagram, or Twitter. You just might have what it takes to launch a successful startup and take it from nothing to a global company in your lifetime.

Follow the advice of Napoleon Hill, who said, "Cherish your visions and your dreams, as they are the children of your soul; the blueprints of your ultimate achievements." Heed the counsel of Brian Tracy, who advises, "All successful people, men and women, are big dreamers. They imagine what their future could be, ideal in every respect, and then they work every day toward their distant vision, that goal or purpose."

Over the years, I've learned that "a job well begun is a job half done." Getting started is the hardest part of completing any task or assignment. Writing that first sentence is the most difficult part of finishing a project (like this book). Overcoming inertia and getting started is simple – but it isn't easy. The NIKE motto doesn't say Just Think About It or Just Dream About It or Just Plan It. Take a page from NIKE's book and Just Do It.

The longest journey begins with a single step. We cannot finish the races we do not run. Runners start with a 5K, graduate to a 10K, and train for even longer distances before tackling a marathon. Life is no less a marathon, and developing our Persistence muscles is no less a feat of endurance. Starting now, take that first step toward the successful life you (or you and your partner) envisioned in the first chapter. Get started, then be persistent, and you'll finish what you start. You'll get, and live, the life you deserve.

Quitters Never Win

The secret is not following the right path, it's following
that right path to the end. Don't quit, my friend,
until you've arrived."
– Toni Sorenson

"There are two fatal errors that keep great
projects from coming to life:
1) Not finishing
2) Not starting"
– Buddha Gautama

YOUR DEFINITION OF successful living will change. What you envision as successful living today may bear little resemblance to successful living as you define it five, ten, twenty, or more years from today. You can always alter your vision, edit your dreams, and refine your success definition—they're yours. And you, or you and your partner, can change them. But if success is your goal, what you cannot do is not have them. And once you have them, your vision will neither be realized nor your dreams fulfilled if you yield to disappointment. Your hopes will remain unsatisfied and your goals unaccomplished if you surrender to adversity. On that you can rely.

To experience success as you define it, you must never give in, never give up, never surrender. You can certainly rest, but you must not quit. Quitters never win, and winners never quit. Elite Daily.com ("The Voice of Generation Y" - check out the "Life" section from time to time) has an excellent "in a nutshell" lesson entitled "Quitters Never Win: 3 Things to Remember Before Throwing in the Towel." Here are a few highlights from that online resource. "Why do so many people quit on their goals? The answer is simple: It's easy. The harder choice would be to push through the obstacles and the challenges. Facts are in, more people will fail at success than succeed. More people will fail at their fitness goals . . . fail at their marriages . . . fail in college than succeed. The failure rate at anything and everything seems to be higher than the success rate. It comes down to one thing: Those who make it just never quit and those who don't quit too soon."

The article goes on suggest that most people fail and quit right before their biggest breakthrough or crowning achievement. "Often," the author, Sandy El-Reyes says, "there was just one more stop needed." El-Reyes advises us to remember three key points before quitting. "Remind yourself what you're going back to; remind yourself that most people would quit; remind yourself that the bigger the challenge, the bigger the reward." Read the entire article. It contains great content and inspiring quotes.

Want to be so inspired that you keep on keeping on, despite the obstacles and setbacks, in the face of adversity and disappointment? Read books authored by the great sales professionals of our time. Surely no field of endeavor is more challenging than sales. And whether or not you earn your livelihood by offering products or services for sale in exchange for a commission, you are most certainly "in sales." Every day, you're selling your ideas, your beliefs, yourself. Read the works of Tom Hopkins or Brian Tracy and glean their insights into how the great sales professionals, of our time or any time, have learned to "never" quit.

The Mackay MBA of Selling in the Real World (by Harvey Mackay) has been beneficial to our company's staff who have front-line sales relationships with our clients and customers. The book is a compendium of real-world lessons that span Mackay's long and storied sales career. Read Chapter 36, "There's No Education Like Adversity." On page 302 of this work, Mackay quotes John D. Rockefeller as saying, "I do not think there is any other quality so essential to success of any kind as the quality of perseverance." That same page tells the story of Theodor Geisel. Geisel "wrote 47 books that have sold more than 100 million copies in 18 languages. What most people don't know about Dr. Cat-in-the-Hat Seuss is that he didn't write his first book until he was 33 and it was rejected by 28 publishers before Vanguard Press picked it up."

Mackay adds this point about why quitters never win. "The line between failure and success is so fine that we scarcely know when we pass it—so fine that we are often on the line itself and do not know it. How many people have thrown up their hands at a time when a little more effort, a little more patience would have achieved success?"

I highly recommend reading Angela Duckworth's Grit – The Power of Passion and Perseverance. Her scientific treatise—extensively researched, well written, and highly informative—sets forth a compelling case for the power of persistence. Here's the back cover summary. "Why do naturally gifted people frequently fail to reach their potential while others with far less talent go on to achieve amazing things? The secret to outstanding achievement is not talent but a special blend of passion and persistence called 'grit.' Duckworth shows how our inclination to revere natural talent is misguided; in terms of achievement, the effort we put in and our reaction to setbacks count for far more . . . 'grit' is something that can be learned and offers a new formula for outstanding individual and collective success."

Full Speed Ahead

"Damn the torpedoes, full speed ahead."
– Admiral Farragut

THIS ORDER WAS given by David Glasgow Farragut, rear admiral, vice admiral, and admiral in the US Navy, when engaged in the Battle of Mobile Bay (an August 5th, American Civil War encounter). This idiomatic phrase suggests that we press on toward victory, regardless of the odds and despite the challenges. On March 4, 1933, newly elected US President Franklin Delano Roosevelt included the now-famous words, "The only thing we have to fear is fear itself" in his inaugural address. At the time, the United States was facing one of the worst economic crises in history and FDR, the eternal optimist, was trying his best to keep the country from erupting in panic. Is "fear itself" that debilitating, paralyzing force that keeps us from trying; or, when we try and fail, keeps us from persisting; or when we persist and meet with adversity, keeps us from persevering until we succeed?

If not fear, is it laziness that keeps us from accomplishing all that we might and all that we can? Sloth, after all, is one of the seven deadly sins. Perhaps it is sloth that keeps us from getting started; or if we get started, keeps us from continuing; or if we continue, allows us to give up and give in to weariness and fatigue.

If it's neither fear nor laziness, could it be a "lack of will" that comes between us and what we say we want – between us and what we believe we could have and should do? Sure, we'd "like" to be successful, but only if succeeding isn't really all that hard. Of course, we want what we want, but we want the getting of it to be easy and the keeping of it just a walk in the park.

For every "I should," there are a million "yes, buts." I should exercise . . . yes, but: the gym is so far—it's probably really crowded – people might make fun of me—I'm going to be so sore—I can work out at home—and so on and so on. For every "I want," there are a million "what ifs." I want to be a millionaire, but what if I fail—what if I go broke—what if I lose my shirt—what if I have to pay a fortune in taxes—what if my kids become drug addicts—what if I have to sacrifice my home life and I end up alone! We borrow trouble every step of the way. We're so focused on the torpedoes that we lose sight of the sea.

This is your time —today is your day. You cannot anticipate all the difficulties you'll encounter or predict the challenges you'll surely face. But, if you think you can and if you persist and never surrender, you can overcome. You will succeed if you believe you will. You must get up and get going if you want "it" badly enough. Damn the torpedoes, FULL SPEED AHEAD!

Personal Success Strategies for Persistent and Determined Living

1. On a scale of 1 to 10, with 1 being easily discouraged and lacking follow-through, and 10 being "always" finishing what I start, despite the obstacles, setbacks, or disappointments, generally, how persistent am I? _____

2. When I reflect on the importance of persistence, here are at least three recent (within the past 12 months) situations I can recall in which I successfully demonstrated this critical quality.

3. In the past year, I can identify the following 3–5 primary reason(s) I've forsaken a project, given up on a goal, or lost interest in an objective.

Of these obstacles, the one most consistently difficult for me to overcome is:

4. These are the three key goals I would most like to accomplish, personally and/or professionally, over the next 12 months:

5. I will be persistent, determined, and focused in accomplishing my goals and meeting my objectives. Here are some strategies that will help me overcome the inevitable distractions, manage competing priorities, and move past potential discouragement.

6. I will internalize the quality of persistence to help ensure my success each and every day. I will demonstrate my persistence and show my determination in all of the following ways:

Chapter 4

The Third "P" = Principles

"I love those who can smile in trouble, who can gather strength from distress and grow brave by reflection.

'Tis the business of little minds to shrink, but they whose heart is firm, and whose conscience approves their conduct, will pursue their principles unto death."

– Attributed to both Leonardo da Vinci and Thomas Paine

THE ONLINE BUSINESS Dictionary defines principles as "fundamental norms, rules or values that represent what is desirable and positive for a person, group, organization or community, and help it in determining the rightfulness or wrongfulness of its actions." You've heard the old adage "If you don't stand for something, you'll fall for anything." You can explore the lineage of this quote on the online resource, Quote Investigator—it has an interesting history.

Principles are what you stand for; the thoughts and behaviors you regard as right and just and fair. The words "Values," "Ethics," and "Morals" have similar meanings, but for our purposes, and because it's a "P" word, we'll use the term "Principles" to incorporate all of these concepts.

Google the term "universal values" and you'll find the concept "moral universalism." This term, also called "moral objectivism," suggests that "for all similarly situated individuals, regardless of culture, race, sex, religion, nationality, sexual orientation, or any other distinguishing feature, there is a shared set of values. These values include Right Conduct, Peace, Truth, Love and Non-violence." Another online universal moral values list includes Trustworthiness, Respect, Responsibility, Fairness, Caring, and Citizenship. A third version of purported "Basic Values" includes Honesty, Fairness, Loyalty, Sharing, Solidarity, Civility, Respect, and Consideration. This source sets forth the position that "these basic values make it possible for every human to realize or maintain life, love and happiness." Finally, The United Nations has adopted this Universal Values List: Peace, Freedom, Social Progress, Equal Rights, and Human Dignity.

There's more "alikeness" in these lists, in my view, than there are differences. While not all cultures or religions or peoples across the globe will agree on the day-to-day way in which these principles, or values, are behaviorally demonstrated, it's my view that some value-laden concepts are so basic, so compelling as to be universally accepted and endorsed. These principles include the ethical and moral human qualities identified and set forth in the preceding paragraph.

Your personal principles may be grounded in religious faith, but they don't have to be. They may have been instilled in you by your parents and family from an early age, or you may have developed your own set of principles through experience and observation, through reading and study. You may be able to articulate your principles, or perhaps you've never given the subject much thought. You may live your life so that it aligns with your sense of right and wrong, or you may espouse one view of the principled ("right") way to live and behave in ways that are contrary to those principles ("wrong").

Hypocrisy is, in essence, living an unprincipled life. The dictionary defines hypocrisy as "the practice of claiming to have moral standards or beliefs to which one's own behavior does not conform; pretense." This chapter suggests that behaving in ways that consistently violate one's personal principles, or are contrary to what we now understand to be universal human values, is the antithesis of real and lasting success.

This chapter also makes the case that principled living as an essential ingredient to successful living. Socrates suggested that "the unexamined life is not worth living." I suggest that the unprincipled life may not worth living either. In exploring the importance of principled living, we're asking whether an unprincipled person (or family or company or organization) can achieve true and lasting success. The balance of this chapter, and your work at the end of it, seeks to answer that important question.

Clarify Your Values

"All decision-making is a values-clarifying exercise."
– Tony Robbins

WHAT DO YOU stand for? It's a simple yet profound question. Values are defined as "a person's principles or standards of behavior; one's judgment of what is important in life." However you form them, and whether or not you are conscious of them, you have established a set of values—principles and standards of behavior that might be called your "conscience." You have an inner sense of when your actions are aligned with your values (your conscience tells you you're acting rightly) or when your values and actions are misaligned (your conscience tells you you're acting wrongly).

What actions, behaviors, or attitudes do you regard as "right"? What constitutes "wrong" in your judgment? Robert Fulghum's book All I Really Need to Know I Learned in Kindergarten was first published in 1986. Since that date, the book has sold more than seven million copies. Here are a few sentences from Fulghum's Kindergarten Lessons that, in my view, have values implications.

"Share everything. Play fair.
Don't hit people.
Put things back where you found them. Clean up your own mess.
Don't take things that aren't yours.
Say you're sorry when you hurt somebody.
When you go out into the world . . . stick together.
Live a balanced life."

Fulghum suggests, "Everything you need to know is in there somewhere. Take any of these items and extrapolate it into sophisticated adult terms and apply it to your family life or your work or government or your world and it holds true and clear and firm." There are other good and basic rules, but I've chosen not to repeat them here. For a full list, consult Fulghum's original work or the 2003 Anniversary Book edition.

Perhaps these early lessons, learned by most of us through our families or our schools or our religious institutions, are a good starting point for articulating your personal values. Generosity, fairness, kindness, honesty, caring, and social consciousness—do you value these qualities? Organization, cleanliness, order—are these attributes important to you? At the end of this chapter, you'll be asked to explore your values, and then to list the 5-7 principles or standards that have the most meaning to you. In all likelihood, your principles and values statement will be unique. You may want to begin that process now by reflecting on the question that opened this section—what do you stand for?

In preparing for our company's annual Team Retreat a few years back, I incorporated Chris Edmonds' book The Culture Engine into my preparation and presentation. The book is aptly subtitled A Framework for Driving Results, Inspiring Employees and Transforming Your Workplace. Chapter 2 of this work, "It Starts with You," lays out a step-by-step process for gaining values clarity. Edmonds first step is "Clarify Your Purpose," followed by "Clarify Your Personal Values and Aligned Behaviors." He follows those steps with "Define Your Values" and "Add Observable, Tangible, Measurable Behaviors to Each Value." While Edmond's work is a primer in company or corporate leadership, it is no less useful as a tool for individual values clarification. I would encourage you to read the book, and to complete the Chapter 2 exercises. I have, and you may find value in doing so as well.

Whether you clarify your values using Edmond's format, completing the Principled Living strategies exercise presented at the end of this chapter, or through some other values clarification format (you may have searched out and found on your own) is of little consequence. You may decide to use no prescribed format at all, and simply write, in free form, a personal "credo" by which you'll choose to live. What matters is that you embrace the concept that values matter and gain the benefits of living a principled life.

Be True to Yourself

"When you fight yourself to discover the real you,
there is only one winner."
– Stephen Richards

"For every one person who praises you, there are a hundred
who would criticize. Heed neither the one for the hundred.
It is your own Opinion that truly matters."
– Richelle E. Goodrich, Slaying Dragons

IN SHAKESPEARE'S PLAY Hamlet, the character Polonius offers these last words of advice to his son, Laertes: "This above all: to thine own self be true, and it must follow, as the night the day, thou canst not then be false to any man." Credit contemporary American author Jennifer DeLucy, with this statement: "If nothing else in this long and short life, let me be true to my conscience, to the dignity of my own heart. Let me act in a way that says I have honored my spirit, as truly as I have honored others'. Let me stand tall and rooted as a mountain in the face of a quaking world." Finally, Dr. Steve Maraboli, billed on his own web site as "the most quoted man alive," (as well as life-changing speaker, best-selling author, behavioral scientist, personal coach, business strategist, and social philosopher) provided this observation: "A lot of the conflict you have in your life exists simply because you're not living in alignment; you're not being true to yourself."

You know how it feels when a car's wheels are out of alignment. The vehicle is difficult to control—pulling to the left or to the right—needing constant correction to stay on track. The ride is rough and bumpy. The journey is more difficult and less comfortable than it needs to be. According to the website "Learn How to Take Care of Your Car Yourself," your misaligned car "has to work much harder to move forward and more fuel is burned than normal. Not only is it dangerous to drive on uneven tires, it also means you have to purchase new tires sooner. With badly aligned wheels, you are taking on unnecessary risk. A little money once in a while getting your wheels aligned can bring you peace of mind." And finally, "Having a car with badly aligned wheels also leads" (to a whole host) "of other connected problems." And the average cost of a wheel alignment? Depending on the car you drive and the mechanic you choose, easily less than $100. So why would we, as relatively intelligent, responsible people, drive on misaligned tires?

More importantly, why would we live a misaligned life? With an improperly aligned life, it's certainly more difficult and requires much more energy to move forward. Living an out-of-alignment life exposes us to untold risks—those we anticipate and choose to disregard, and those we don't even recognize until, too often, it's too late. And the average cost of living a principled life—absolutely nothing!

Sure, you might miss out on an experience others are having. Good for you, if you decide to pass on something you know you shouldn't be doing anyway. Maybe the backstabbers and backbiters will ridicule you when you stand up for your principles and demonstrate principled behavior. Good for you, because many others will hold you up as an example of what a person "should do" and how an individual "ought to behave." And when the misaligned see their lives go off track, their families dissolve, their companies falter, and their health go down the tubes, maybe you'll be the one that shows how the well-aligned life is a source of strength and power. You have the opportunity to demonstrate, by example, that principled living is successful living.

When you and I are behaving in ways that align with our principles and values, we're at peace with ourselves, our families, our coworkers, and our communities. Others trust in us, believe in us, and "like" us. In the work environment, people want us on their team. If we're team leaders, our colleagues want to align themselves with us and follow our example. They appreciate our principled efforts and want to see us succeed. If we own or operate a company, people want to do business with us, and will encourage others to do business with us as well. Be true to yourself and reap the amazing rewards of principled living.

Let Your Conscience Be Your Guide

"It's easier to fight an army than to fight your conscience."
– Matshona Dhilwayo

"Man cannot suffer more than from a guilty conscience."
– Eraldo Banovac

THE 1940 DISNEY movie "Pinocchio" gave us sound advice for acting in accordance with our principles. If you know the story, Pinocchio, to his detriment, didn't always follow Jiminy Cricket's advice. It's a simple tale, illustrative of the perils of acting contrary to conscience. It tells a story of second chances and redemption, and ultimately, of the rewards of acting rightly. Jiminy, acting as Pinocchio's conscience, offers wise counsel in song. I encourage you to locate and listen to the original recording which suggests "Always Let Your Conscience Be Your Guide."

Pangs of conscience, "feelings of shame, guilt or embarrassment resulting from behavior which one regrets," really hurt. The psychological and sometimes physical wounds caused when we act in ways that are contrary to the dictates of conscience are difficult to heal. "I really wish I hadn't done that" . . . "If only I'd have chosen a different path" . . . and rarely, if ever, do we get a second chance. Regret is a bitter pill to swallow. The damage to our spirits cannot be undone. The "sore spot" can heal, but the scar tissue is still there. Collateral damage done to those who love and trust us (when the "bad" act breaches trust or breaks a promise) can last a lifetime. Guilt is a terrible burden. The best remedy for guilt and shame is avoidance. Act, to the greatest extent humanly possible, in ways congruent with your principles.

In the real world, though, we all falter and fail to do what we know is right—or, worse, make a conscious choice to do what we know is wrong. Sometimes, our bad behavior is never discovered. Not being "found out" can make us act better, thanking our lucky stars that, although we may feel guilt, we were not subjected to the shame and embarrassment that "public" misbehavior can bring. Sometimes being found out leads to turning over of a new leaf. Vowing never to risk putting ourselves in that position again, we may beg forgiveness, seek counseling, ask for treatment, change our habits, and alter our behaviors. Alternatively, success in keeping unprincipled behavior secret may embolden the bad actor. If you persist in acting badly—of this you can be sure—ultimately, eventually, inevitably, your "sins will find you out." It's not a question of if you'll get caught, it's only a matter of when. One of our team members says this cautionary statement was often made in her family: "Be careful of the things you do in the dark—they'll always find their way into the light."

One very public example of a good and successful man acting badly in my community is former University of Texas head baseball coach Augie Garrido. Google Coach Garrido, and you'll discover that he was suspended from his head coaching position for drunken driving. According to a June 23, 2009 Associated Press article, "Garrido was arrested in the early morning hours last Saturday near Austin's downtown entertainment district. "I made a serious mistake," Garrido said at a news conference regarding the incident. "I drank alcohol, I got behind the wheel of a car, and that's a bad decision."

Perhaps the most public Austin meltdown, at least in relatively recent history, is the misadventure of the Travis County district attorney, Rosemary Lehmberg. Arrested for DUI in 2013, Ms. Lehmberg's story was the lead television report and newspaper headline that April. And although she was neither terminated nor required to resign from office, holding the DA's position until 2017, Ms. Lehmberg's behavior was another woeful example of "do as I say, not as I do".

There are many more such cautionary tales—in my town and my state, in your town and your state—in our nation and around the world. Scandalous sagas illustrating unprincipled acting proliferate, especially around election season. Sometimes it's alcohol, other times it's sex, sometimes both. Unprincipled acting may involve theft, larceny, embezzlement—or something else altogether. Bill Clinton's infamous line "I did not have sex with that woman" still echoes as one of the greatest lies in history. While the bad acting didn't compromise national security or cause a crash on Wall Street, it embarrassed and hurt the Clinton family, damaged the Democratic Party, and tainted the presidency. We've not yet seen what lasting and deleterious effect a Trump presidency, regarded by many Americans as "unprincipled", may have on the Republican Party, our country, and the world.

The most recent example of unprincipled, unscrupulous, scandalous public misconduct is the sordid Jeffrey Epstein story. A July 2, 2020 Town&Country article (https://townandcountrymag.com/society/money-and-power/a28352055/), by Caroline Hallemann, "What we Do and Don't Know About Jeffrey Epstein", opens with these words. "The financier, who had ties to celebrities, politicians, and royalty, was arrested last year (2019) on multiple disturbing charges. He died by suicide in jail", (allegedly, although many doubts and uncertainties about the official suicide ruling remain), "but questions about his life and crimes still remain."

In 2009, Hallman tells us, Epstein pleaded guilty to a felony charge of solicitation of prostitution involving a minor, and was sentenced to 18 months in prison. He served 13 months of that sentence, was granted a work release, and was allowed to commute to an office outside the jail six days a week. He also registered as a sex offender. Yet his associations with the rich and powerful continued, as did, from what we've heard and what we've read, his licentious conduct. The fallout from Epstein's unprincipled sexual misconduct will not only haunt his victims for a lifetime, but may have lingering implications for previous friends and associates, no matter how hard they try to distance themselves from him and his immoral legacy.

No list of unprincipled acts, public and private, would be complete without a reference to one of today's most pervasive scandals—sexual harassment. Both within and outside the workplace, unwanted sexual advances, more typically than not perpetrated by male authority figures on less-powerful female victims, has reached epidemic proportions. Leonard Pitts Jr., Columnist for the Miami Herald and reprinted in the Austin-American Statesman, said this (published in the Statesman on Sunday, June 17, 2018): "Have we not yet learned our lesson? Are we not yet ready to take seriously the pain of our daughters, wives, sisters and mothers? With Harvey Weinstein, Matt Lauer, Roy Moore, Scott Baio, Morgan Freeman, Louis C.K., Glenn Thrush, Charlie Rose, John Conyers, R. Kelly, Ben Affleck, Donald Trump, George H. W. Bush and dozens of other famous men standing accused of various degrees of sexual misconduct, with Bill O'Reilly unemployed, Bill Cosby facing prison, and Bill Clinton once again stumbling over Monica Lewinsky, it should be clear that the era of women suffering in silence and humiliation is over."

Countless women who once endured their pain in silence are speaking out and speaking up. Their tormentors are being found out and their transgressions are becoming widely known. Some perpetrators are being censured and embarrassed, perhaps alienated, at least for a time, from their families and loved ones. And for what? The once-small "snowflake" "Me Too" movement has become an avalanche that no one can ignore. Perhaps all the men named by Pitts, and those who are less famous or whose bad acting has not yet been discovered, will follow the AAA steps outlined below.

If you act in an unprincipled way, regardless of the offense, take an AAA approach – Admit, Apologize, and Atone. Admit the misconduct and deal with the consequences. You'll save yourself a lot of grief in the long run. Lying to prevent being found out, as we all know too well, is a very slippery slope. One cover-up lie requires another, and then a bigger one, and so and so on . . . it's emotionally and physically draining. Avoid the riptide that pulls you down and holds you under. Confess and come clean.

If your unprincipled behavior has harmed another, apologize and ask for forgiveness. A sincere, heartfelt apology, delivered with true humility, begins the healing process—for you and for those you may have wronged. Keep your promise to be better and do better.

After the admission and apology, Atone for the unprincipled act. Atonement means making reparations for the wrong. Making it right, whatever that means in the context of the unprincipled act, builds on the healing process and sets the stage for true recovery. Do what's right to repair the damage done and regain your self-respect.

There's one more step for full recovery from unprincipled acts of commission or omission. Learn from your "mistakes"—vow not to repeat them—and let them go. Forgive yourself. Recognize that you want to "do better" and that you can "do better," and then "do better." There's nothing to be gained by beating yourself up over past acts that, once done, cannot be undone. Look toward a more principled future, and reap the many, many rewards of acting rightly, as you define "the right." And always let your conscience be your guide!

Personal Success Strategies for Principled Living

"If you have a compass, you won't get lost at sea.
If you have a conscience, you won't get lost in life."
– Matshona Dhilwayo

1. What do I stand for? What principles do I hold as absolute and inviolable?

2. What behaviors do my values "demand" that I exhibit? How do family, friends, and associates know my values by my actions?

3. What attitudes and behaviors would violate my principles and compromise my values?

4. On a scale of 1 to 10, with 1 being thinking and behaving in ways that are "totally inconsistent" with my values and 10 being "perfectly aligned" with the dictates of my conscience, where would I rank my adherence to principle? _____

5. Here is a list of three (or more) specific "things" I can do or "things" I can stop doing that will bring my daily life into closer alignment with my principles and values:

6. How will my life improve by doing (or not doing) the things I've listed above?

7. If I have unresolved feelings of guilt, shame, or embarrassment for unconscionable behavior, what will I do, specifically, and when, exactly, to regain my self-respect and peace of mind through the AAA (Admit, Apologize, and Atone) approach?

Remember These Truths

"Listen to your conscience. You have to live with
yourself for the rest of your life."
– Frank Sonnenberg

"Follow Your Conscience. Sleep well."
– Frank Sonnenberg

Chapter **5**

The First "E" = Energy

> "Without passion, you don't have energy; without energy, you have nothing."
> - Donald Trump

> "Passion is energy. Feel the power that comes from focusing on what excites you."
> - Oprah Winfrey

IT'S NOT LIKELY we'd find two more disparate contemporary figures than Donald Trump and Oprah Winfrey. Yet the quotes that open this chapter vividly demonstrate the virtually universal agreement about the power of **Energy**. Our society is just short of rabid in its energy pursuit. Red Bull, Monster, Rockstar . . . In 2017 (https://www.statsa.com/statistics/558022/us-energy-drink-sales/) energy drinks accounted for 30 percent of the dollar sales of packaged beverages sold in the U. S. And sales have been increasing every year. Google "energy supplements," and you'll discover an astounding array of "natural" and artificial products promising to "rev up your metabolism and make you feel like you have more physical and mental energy." What's wrong with this picture? Is energy really "out there"? Can you swallow it in a pill or drink it from a can? I believe that you cannot.

Instead of making Passion a 4th P, I've chosen to make its end product, Energy, the first E. As Trump and Winfrey suggest, Energy and Passion are two sides of the same coin. And with Energy and Passion come another important E, Enthusiasm—without which, as Ralph Waldo Emerson suggests, nothing great was ever achieved!

Powerful, long-lasting energy, in my view and experience, is produced by the mind, heart and spirit, and only fleetingly and superficially by caffeine, ginseng, amino acids, or Vitamin B-12. I'm not judging whether those substances, and others like them, are good or bad for us. These and many other energy products have been declared safe for human consumption, and according to their users, have positive physical or psychological effects, so where's the harm? If something in a can or bottle makes us feel or think we can "plow another round," endure another twenty minutes on the treadmill, or pull an all-nighter when the situation warrants, then what's the problem?

Nothing, perhaps, except that the quick fix never lasts. And the easy way is illusory at best, and at worst, counterproductive. Passion—for a cause, a profession, a goal, a business, or even another person—is an abundant supply of incredible energy. And the energy derived from passion is free and inexhaustible. It's an energy that enables us to meet our goals and accomplish our objectives. The energy that flows from the passionate pursuit of what's important to us is an essential ingredient in successful living.

Get Up and Get Going

"The longer I live, the more deeply I am convinced that that which makes the difference between one man and another—between the weak and the powerful, the great and the insignificant, is energy—invisible determination—a purpose once formed and then death or victory."
– Sir Thomas Buxton

"The world belongs to the energetic."
– Ralph Waldo Emerson

DO YOU GREET each new day with energy and enthusiasm? Are you so passionate about what you're doing at work that you can't wait to see how much you can accomplish? Do you tackle your "to do" list with gleeful anticipation or approach the day's work with apprehension— or worse, with indifference? Do you enjoy your coworkers and look forward to chatting with them about what they're up to, professionally or personally? Are you excited about "getting up and getting going" on Monday morning? Or do you find yourself continually hitting the proverbial snooze button and sleepwalking through the week until five o'clock Friday?

Studies show that most of the world's workers are either actively unhappy or passively disengaged at work. What a pity! Work is where you're likely to spend 35% or more of your roughly 5,840 annual waking hours. Based on 8 working hours x 5 workdays per week x 50 weeks (take 2 weeks of well-deserved vacation), you'll work roughly 2000 hours each year—not counting your daily commute or the time you may spend thinking about work when you're away from the workplace.

Not everyone has a "dream job." We're not all athletes or Hollywood superstars, business moguls, or titans of industry. If you're not doing what you love, you have options. Go back to school and qualify yourself for the job you'd like to be doing—explore other industries that might be a better fit for your interests, talents, and abilities—do what you've been doing, but change your work environment for someplace more to your liking or closer to home—start a business of your own. Choose . . . to do things differently, or to do different things. After all, it's up to you.

Think about your best day at work, a day when everything went your way and for a time, however brief it might have been, you felt good about yourself and what you were doing. You felt valued and appreciated, capable and productive. Decide to feel that way again . . . start off slow— capture that feeling at work for 30 minutes every day . . . then feel great about your job for an hour. Love your job every morning or every afternoon . . . then DECIDE to fall in love with what you do all day, every day.

Unless your current work environment is so toxic that it adversely affects your mental health or psychological well-being, choosing to love what you do can only help you. Passion for the work that you do dramatically increases your success potential and contributes greatly to your overall happiness. Kahlil Gibran, author of The Prophet, offered profound observations regarding work. His thoughts can be quickly found online. Now might be a good time to read them. I hope they resonate with you, as they do with me.

Maybe you're fortunate enough not to "have to" earn your daily bread. I suggest that passion-fueled energy is no less crucial and perhaps is even more important to you. Maybe you can't work, for one reason or another—no worries—if you're reading this book, you likely have the ability to be productive in some capacity, and if so, to feel and demonstrate passion for what interests, fascinates, compels, or inspires you.

Are you passionate about volunteer work in a charitable organization or in your community of faith? Do you gain satisfaction from participating in a group or individual sport or activity, or watching your child excel at school, on the practice field, or in marching band? It doesn't matter what motivates, stimulates, moves, or excites you . . . It only matters that something does. Passion creates energy—and energy fuels accomplishment. Whatever you "have" to do or whatever you "want" to do, get up and get going!

Exercise is an essential part of getting up and getting going. Surveys show that the average American spends five hours a day watching television. We sit at our jobs, come home and eat, then sit on our sofas or lounge in our easy chairs and switch on the TV. The inertia and inactivity that fills many of our lives is not only unproductive but deadly. We are, quite literally, killing ourselves with too much sitting.

If you have a desk job, as many of us do, get up and get going. Take the stairs. Park farther from the door. Include a 20-minute walk in your daily lunch routine. Consider a stand-up desk. At home, put the treadmill, or any of the countless QVC or Home Shopping Channel exercise options, in the TV room.

Exercising doesn't tire you; it gives you energy. Go online and search "How does exercise give you energy?" You'll discover that regular exercise does much more than energize. The Mayo Clinic web site lists these seven benefits of regular exercise. "Exercise: controls weight; combats health conditions and diseases; improves mood; boosts energy; promotes better sleep; puts the spark back into your sex life, and finally, exercise can be fun." Most experts recommend no less exercise than 30 minutes 3 times per week for healthy adults. If you need to lose weight or have other specific health-related issues, check with a health professional and learn what's right for you. Get up and get going!

Live Healthy

"To ensure good health: eat lightly, breathe deeply,
live moderately, cultivate cheerfulness,
and maintain an interest in life."
– William Londen

"To keep the body in good health is a duty . . . otherwise we
shall not be able to keep the mind strong and clear."
– Buddha

HEALTHY LIVING IS about more than eating our vegetables or shopping in the organic foods section. It's more than drinking room-temperature bottled water or avoiding red meat. These practices may indeed be healthy, but healthy living is as much, or more, about what we think as it is about what we do—or for that matter, what we don't do.

We've got one body—one brain, one heart, and one liver—two eyes, ears, kidneys, arms, hands, legs, and feet. We're blessed to live in an age where medical science has advanced to the point that our extremities can be replaced with fully functional prosthetic devices. Some of our "parts" can be replaced through transplant—life-giving organs donated by family, friends, or strangers. Bone marrow transplants help those with diseases like leukemia and anemia. A diseased liver can be replaced by just a piece of a living donor's healthy organ. (An entire liver may be transplanted, or just a section. The liver is the only body part able to regenerate, so a transplanted portion of the liver can rebuild to normal capacity within weeks—isn't this a wonder!)

Absent extreme circumstances, where the wonders of modern medicine or the bonds of family or the kindness of friends or the generosity of strangers comes to the rescue, we are born with all our bodily parts. We're responsible, throughout our adult life, for their care. We're accountable for choosing to eat right and exercise. We're responsible for protecting our bodies from drug and alcohol abuse. We're answerable for scheduling regular checkups and seeking help when we're ill or when we sense a change in our bodily functions. We're responsible for brushing our teeth and maintaining good oral hygiene – for washing our hands and drinking our water. It's we who must take prescribed life-sustaining medications or alter high-health-risk behaviors. It's all up to us.

Healthy living depends on doing all the basics—eating right, exercising regularly, and getting the rest that we need. Healthy living further demands that we refrain from doing those things—smoking, abusing drugs or alcohol, engaging in unsafe sexual behavior – that that are known to damage our health, rob us of joy, and which, if taken to extremes, pose a risk to our very lives.

We know what's bad for us. We know that no good can come of drug and alcohol abuse, yet substance abuse is the leading cause of preventable illness and death in the United States. We know the health risks associated with obesity, but more than two-thirds of us are overweight as adults, and of those, one-third are considered obese. We know that diabetes and high blood pressure, without proper care and behavior modification, rob their sufferers of health and energy. Untreated and improperly cared for, these maladies, and so many others, will hasten our demise. We know there's a link between poor health and stress, yet we invite stress into our lives by bad acting or bad thinking. And we don't adopt the healthy behaviors and attitudes we know reduce stress and alleviate its harmful effects.

Outside of science fiction, there's no possibility of brain transplant—no neural prosthesis. Beyond any shadow of reasonable doubt, the one brain we have works best when we feed it with positivity. We thrive when we love not only what we do, but those with whom we do it. We're energized when we surround ourselves with positive, like-minded friends and acquaintances. We're uplifted when we're giving, sharing, and kind.

Ralph Waldo Emerson said, "The purpose of life is not to be happy. It is to be useful, to be honorable, to be compassionate, to have it make some difference that you have lived and lived well." In his 2001 book Standing for Something: 10 Neglected Virtues That Will Heal Our Hearts and Homes, Gordon B. Hinckley said, "The best antidote I know for worry is work. The best cure for weariness is the challenge of helping someone who is even more tired. One of the great ironies of life is this: He or she who serves almost always benefits more than he or she who is served." Giving and serving, and supporting and helping are as essential to healthy living as are eating right and exercising regularly.

Nothing in my experience is more rewarding of fulfilling, more energizing than making a positive difference in others' lives. Making a difference doesn't require grand gestures or large monetary donations. Helping isn't always about money or tangible gifts. Time may be the greatest gift any of us can give. Unlike wealth, time is an equitable resource. We each have 24 hours in our days and virtually total control over how we choose to use them. Not-for-profit organizations serve a variety of important purposes and provide a myriad of services. They all need funds to operate. But they also need volunteer involvement, support, and participation. People—and for that matter, animals—who are hurting need food and shelter, to be sure. But they also need encouragement, a listening ear, an understanding smile, a warm blanket, or a simple hug.

Live healthy by caring for yourself physically, in every context. Care for your mental and emotional health by surrounding yourself with the positive and insulating yourself from the negative. Practice random and conscious acts of kindness. Do good works, and enjoy the passion and energy that result.

You Can Rest When You're Dead

"Men do not die from overwork.
They die from dissipation and worry."
– Charles Evans Hughes

"Without work, we die daily."
– Lailah Gifty Akita

"I think in life you should work on yourself
until the day you die."
– Serena Williams

IF YOU'RE UNDER forty, you may think the suggestions in this section don't apply to you. The Rest When You're Dead message is directed primarily toward those who think they're too old to be energized through work or other productive pursuits. But the thoughts in these next few paragraphs apply to anyone at any age involved in any field of endeavor, including volunteerism and full-time parenting.

Throughout our twenties, thirties, and forties, when the foundation for successful living can and should be laid, many of us never fully engage with our work or find fulfillment in other productive pursuits. Some of us labor in fields we don't enjoy with people we don't respect, and regard work as a misfortune. In our fifties, we can't wait for the day we can walk away from work altogether. And sixty, seventy . . . even eighty . . . fugetaboutit!

Far too often, in planning for our financial future, our vision of retirement doesn't include planning for our social and psychological futures. At any and every age, engagement in work or other activities that have meaning, purpose, or are simply pleasurable isn't always a priority. Heed the wise words of Henry Ford: "Anyone who stops learning is old, whether twenty or eighty. Anyone who keeps learning stays young. The greatest thing in life" (and the most energizing thing you can do) "is to keep your mind young".

In 2018, my family celebrated our mother/grandmother/great-grandmother on the occasion of her 90th birthday. Mom worked at our event rental company, Premiere Events, on Wednesdays, and on Saturdays as well, until Dementia robbed her of the pleasure. Did she work because she had to? No indeed! She worked because work is love made visible— she loves me, and she loves her Premiere family. Her work contributed to Premiere. Our customers loved relating to Mary Thomas. Our team adores "Grandma Mary." She's treasured, still today, as a positive influence in our workplace and a remarkable example to everyone with whom she interacted.

Her involvement with Premiere never tired her—she found it energizing. Her work on our behalf didn't exhaust her—it gave her joy and fulfillment. Her only regret was "I wish I could have done more." Leon Edel said, "The answer to old age is to keep one's mind busy and to go on with one's life as if it were interminable." More to the point, keeping one's mind busy is the answer at any age.

My husband, Richard, works every day. Richard works because he needs to, but he doesn't have to. He needs to feel productive—he doesn't need the money. He appreciates being appreciated, and to the maximum extent any of us can, is determined to influence, if not control, his own future. He's actively engaged and fully occupied in the here and now—all the while seeking and seizing the opportunities that interest and excite him. His abilities and consistency and determination are an inspiration to all those who know him. Richard is eighty years young (at this writing). He'll rest when he's dead.

Then there's me. I freely admit I'm an unrepentant workaholic—type Triple A. Chronologically, I've just turned 70—psychologically, I'm somewhere in my forties—fifty, tops. I work forty to fifty hours every week, more or less. If we, Richard and I, are reasonably cautious, fiscally responsible, and manage our assets wisely, we've got all the money we should ever need. I work because what I do is my purpose, my calling, my reason for being. I work because people are my passion—I love and appreciate those for whom we work. I'm grateful and thankful and those who work with me. For me, and I suggest for most of you reading these words, productive work or activity is or should be an integral and indispensable part of living a successful life.

If it weren't Premiere, it would be something equally interesting and rewarding—because what matters is neither the content nor the context of the work, but the attitude toward it. Not the "what" we do, but the sheer joy in doing. Not the task before us, but the satisfaction in a job well done. Work enriches every aspect of my life. I'll rest when I'm dead.

You're as young as you feel. Age truly is just a state of mind. Peruse any internet listing of "Famous Folks Who Launched Careers After Fifty." You'll find the stories of Colonel Sanders (KFC), Laura Ingalls Wilder (Little House on the Prairie) and Ronald Reagan (who first held elected office at age fifty-five). Julia Child's The French Chef debuted nationally in 1963. Julia Child was fifty-one. Ray Kroc was fifty-two when he joined McDonald's, and you know the rest of that story.

Great quotes sometimes come from unexpected sources. Sophia Loren said, "There is a fountain of youth: it is your mind, your talents, the creativity you bring to your life and the lives of people you love. When you learn to tap this source, you will truly have defeated age." Work while you can—live a full life while you can—go and do and achieve and learn and love while you can. Rest when you're dead.

Personal Success Strategies for Energy Optimization

> "It is health that is the real wealth,
> not pieces of gold and silver."
> – Mahatma Gandhi

1. On a scale of 1 to 10, where would I rank myself in terms of my satisfaction with my physical health? _____ What would I like my ranking to be? _____ What specific action steps will I take to live a physically healthier, more energetic lifestyle, and when will I begin?

2. On the same 10-point scale, how much do I agree with the statement "I am engaged in my work and energized by what I do." _____ How engaged and energized would I like to be? _____ What specific steps will I take, and when will I undertake them, in order to derive more satisfaction, enjoyment, and energy from the field in which I labor, the activities in which I engage, and/or the people with whom I associate?

3. If the number 1 is Totally Dissatisfied and the number 10 is Completely Satisfied, what's my level of satisfaction with the time and energy invested in my family, my circle of friends and acquaintances, and my community? _____ What specific acts or behaviors would increase my satisfaction in this aspect of my life?

What am I willing to do, or forsake doing, to derive more energy from my familial, work, and other relationships?

4. **If you're in your twenties, thirties, or forties:** What would I change, today or tomorrow, that would bring me greater energy, joy, and fulfilment in the workplace? What attitudinal, behavioral, environmental, or other changes would help contribute to successful living by my definition?

5. **If you're fifty or older:** If I picture myself ten or fifteen years in the future, what will I do to ensure I remain relevant? What will I do to meet my social and psychological needs (especially if my future plans include conventional notions of retirement)? From where will I derive my sense of purpose, my energy, and my satisfaction?

6. Long term, what does a successful future look like to me from a work standpoint? What am I not doing today that would give me greater energy, leave me feeling energized, and fill me with joy? How, specifically, and by when, exactly can I take the steps (different job, new or improved skills, alternative degree plan or career path, different associates, etc.) that will put me and keep me on the path toward the successful future I've envisioned?

By the way, whatever your age, make sure you've made your end-of-life preparations. If you don't have a will, prepare one. If your will is old and outdated, revise it. If you haven't done your pre-need funeral or memorial (or no funeral, no memorial) planning, do it. Make your wishes known to those closest to you—and put them in written form.

Food for Thought

"Don't go to the grave with your best work
still inside of you. Die empty."
– Todd Henry

"I want to be thoroughly used up when I die, for the harder
I work the more I live. I rejoice in life for its own sake."
– George Bernard Shaw

"It must be good to die in the knowledge that one has done
some truthful work . . . and to know that, as a result, one
will live on in the memory of at least a few and leave a good
example for those who come after."
– Vincent van Gogh

Chapter 6

The Second "E" = Expertise

"Wise people understand the need to consult experts;
only fools are confident they know everything."
– Ken Poirot

TO WHOM DO we listen? Who influences our behavior? Whose counsel do we seek? Most of us are persuaded, to more or less a degree, by "expert" advice from authoritative sources. We seek to imitate and emulate those who have been successful at doing what we want to do or at being what we wish to become. Whether the goal is achieving greater career success; founding and building a successful business; excelling on the football field, baseball diamond, basketball court, or golf course; becoming better marriage partners or parents or getting and staying fit and trim, many of us will attempt to follow an expert's recommendations.

We're conditioned, from birth through life, to heed authority. The words authority and expertise are sometimes used interchangeably, and both those in authority and those with specialized expertise (e.g. physicians, attorneys, accountants, financial advisors, etc.) have influence, if not control, over us, our actions, and our beliefs. We're programmed, neurologically and psychologically, to follow the instructions of those in charge.

As soon as we're able to understand that actions have consequences, we learn that, to attain rewards or avoid punishment, it's wise to follow our parents' directives. As young children, we're pretty sure our parents know everything . . . until we're teenagers and believe they know nothing. At some point in adulthood, particularly when we have children of our own, we typically develop an appreciation for how smart our parents really are. Throughout our school years, teachers and school officials become the symbols of authority and expertise. If we wish to succeed in the educational environment, we must follow their rules and execute their mandates. Sometimes we're fortunate enough to encounter an expert, inspired teacher who can shape a life, alter a course, or help establish a lifelong positive direction. I will forever be indebted to Mrs. Della Craighead, my high school English teacher. If you enjoy the writing style imbedded in this book, the credit is partially hers.

We're taught to be respectful and attentive to societal authorities, the perceived experts on how to behave in a civilized world. We're inspired by the heroism and self-sacrifice of police officers, fire fighters, and other public servants. But run afoul of the law, and even a relatively innocuous offence, handled poorly by the offender or member of the police force, can have deadly consequences. On a commercial airline, failure to follow instructions from a uniformed crew member is a federal offense. If we're unlucky enough to experience trouble in flight, we can only hope to be fortunate enough to be saved from disaster by the expert actions of a dedicated crew and a hero-pilot like Chesley Sullenberger III.

In hierarchical work environments, we comply with established chains of command and lines of communication . . . or risk disciplinary action. There's no doubt that the boss has authority over us and some degree of power to control or influence our future. That's why it's important to seek employment, if working for someone else is your goal, in a company or organization that values individual team members, respects diversity, and offers opportunity. The boss may or may not be an expert but will generally, through credentials, experience, performance, and expertise, have earned the right to be in charge.

You can use the human proclivity to embrace expert advice and authoritative opinion to your advantage in every adult role you choose to play. Want to turn your life around? Listen to someone who has overcome obstacles and triumphed in adversity. Nothing is more inspiring than a school-of-hard-knocks graduate who has achieved lofty goals and realized seemingly impossible dreams. Want to be the one that helps others turn their lives around? Share your story with those who are looking for a positive role model.

Do you want to become as wealthy as Warren Buffet or as influential as Pope Francis? Coach the next Little League World Series champions? Win the Oscar for Best Actress in a Leading Role? Take your place among America's most admired men and women? Whatever you dream of doing, dream of being, or dream of having, chances are someone has already been there and shown the way. The formula by which you must achieve your success and the criteria by which you must demonstrate your expertise are likely well known, documented, and readily available. Learn from the success of others and emulate their winning attitudes, behaviors, and work ethic.

Master Your Trade

"To become a master at any skill, it takes the total effort of your: heart, mind, and soul working together."
– Maurice Young

"You must immerse yourself in your work. You have to fall in love with your work . . . You must dedicate your life to mastering your skill. That's the secret of success."
– Chef Jiro

WHATEVER YOUR FIELD of endeavor, achieving expertise is the golden ticket. The online resource, Entrepreneurs-Journey.com, in an article entitled "How to Become an Expert," suggests that "there are many good reasons why expert status is coveted. Here are some: Being an expert means you're "competent to deliver value" (to your clients, customers, patients, etc.); "being an expert means you're respected by your peers; being an expert means you're qualified to teach others; being an expert means you're able to command premium rates for services you render as an expert."

How do you become an expert in your field? Journalist, author, and educator Michael Bugeja suggests that expertise is achieved through a combination of education and experience. Bugeja says, "Education is a lifelong experience. Experience is a lifelong education. Education plus experience equals expertise."

Unless you're a doctor or other medical professional, attorney or accountant, teacher/professor or pilot or pastor, chances are your classroom learning does not directly relate to what you do today. Earning a bachelor's degree in psychology and sociology didn't prepare me for a specific career or job opportunity, but it did teach me a lot about how and why people think, act, and react. It piqued my interest and made me a lifelong student of human behavior.

Perhaps you chose or will choose a field where there's a more direct correlation between what you study and what you do. Trade and technical schools offer a wide variety of educational and skills training programs that prepare their students for real jobs in the real world. If you've never seen it, watch an episode or two of Blue-Collar Millionaire (which last aired in February, 2017). In its online promotion, CNBC says this. "Some people are born into a rich family and inherit millions of dollars. Other people aren't wealthy by birth and need to work hard to earn their own millions. That latter group can be further divided into white-collar and blue-collar millionaires. It's those blue-collar workers who have worked their way up the money ladder and who are the focus of this half-hour series. The docuseries profiles men and women who have made their fortunes through a can-do mindset and hard work, often having to roll up their sleeves—metaphorically at least, if not literally. The show also highlights how they spend their hard-earned money with having fun off the clock."

When your car won't go or your home heater or air conditioner is on the fritz or there's a plumbing leak, or worse, toilets that won't flush or a sewer that backs up in your home or office, your hero is the person who can fix the problem. Reliable service providers who become skilled technicians and who demonstrate expertise, service excellence and integrity are priceless. Coupling technical skills with business acumen, tradesmen and tradeswomen can and do build successful, impressive, and profitable businesses. You, too, can choose this path to the future you've imagined and the life you deserve.

Other successful individuals have eschewed formal education in favor of any early start on achieving their dreams. Google "successful high school and college dropouts" and you'll find the names of, among others, Steve Jobs, Bill Gates, Walt Disney, and Oprah. There's even an online "dropouts hall of fame." Someday, you may see Chandler Bolt's name included on that list. Chandler is the young (27 as of this writing) mastermind behind Self Publishing School (an invaluable self-publishing resource for those of you interested in authorpreneurship). These and other successful individuals didn't stop learning . . . they just terminated their formal educations. They didn't stop investing in knowledge . . . they just stopped investing in college. They didn't stop honing their crafts, perfecting their skills, or learning from their successes as well as their failures.

Dr. Andres Ericsson's 1990s research on expertise, and subsequent works by Malcolm Gladwell (Outliers) and Geoff Colvin (Talent Is Overrated), suggest that deliberate practice is the key to all extraordinary performance. Anders Ericsson and Robert Pool's book, Peak, Secrets from the New Science of Expertise, is a worthwhile read on this important topic. Whether the goal is mastery of the cello or the game of chess, world-class results require world-class commitment, dedication, and practice. In business, in sports, and in life, the individual who practices best, not necessarily the person who practices longest, is generally the better performer.

PM EZine, the online Performance Management Magazine, makes this claim regarding mastering your trade through practice: "While there is a high correlation between hours of practice and activity during practice, it is not perfect." The two words "deliberate" and "practice" are in fact essential, but it is the conditions that surround both of these words that provide the real boost for turning average performers into world-class performers.

The article continues, "For a simple example, consider the activity of two basketball players practicing free throws for one hour. Player A shoots 200 practice shots. Player B shoots 50. Player B retrieves his own shots, dribbles leisurely, and takes several breaks to talk to friends. Player A has a colleague who retrieves the ball after each attempt. The colleague keeps a record of shots made. If the shot is missed the colleague records whether the miss was short, long, left or right, and the shooter reviews the results after every 10 minutes of practice. To characterize their hour of practice as equal would hardly be accurate. Assuming this is typical of their practice routine and they are equally skilled at the start, which would you predict would be the better shooter after only 100 hours of practice?"

PM Ezine concludes, "Repetition alone, outside of a deliberate plan by which consequences are applied, is not sufficient. It is the conditions that surround the repetitive practice . . . What is important is the feedback and the reinforcement for improvement associated with the repetitions that make the difference."

Huffpost Books provides an excerpt from Daniel Goldman's book Focus: The Hidden Driver of Excellence. These thoughts are included in that work: "How experts in any domain pay attention while practicing makes a crucial difference . . . experts never rest their concentration during active practice. Learning how to improve any skill . . . requires our paying attention. Paying full attention seems to boost the mind's processing speed, strengthen synaptic connections, and expand or create neural networks for what we are practicing. The experts keep paying attention. They concentrate on moves they have yet to perfect, on what's not working in their game, and on refining their mental models of how to play the game."

Take what you've read so far in this section and conduct an online search for "How Does Steph Curry Practice?" This amazing basketball player, and most accurate 3-point shooter of all time, is the poster child for mastering your trade through education. He's an exemplary student of basketball and master of deliberate practice, as are Super-Bowl Champion football quarterbacks Tom Brady, Drew Brees, and Patrick Mahomes II in their game.

Similar insights also appear in the previously referenced Peak. I encourage you to read that work if establishing specialized expertise in the field of your choosing has relevance for you and your success definition. Ericsson's and Pool's work shows us so clearly why so few reach the pinnacle of performance in their fields. Success in any field of endeavor and establishing expertise in the workplace (in whatever context that may be) is amazingly difficult and demanding work.

What more can you do to master your trade and establish your expertise? At the end of this chapter, you'll have the opportunity to answer this all-important question and chart the course for becoming an expert in what you do.

Keep Current and Stay Relevant in Your Chosen Field

"I feel pressured to stay relevant. To stay interesting and interested. To stay at the top of my game and expand."
- Rob Lowe

"The relevant question is not simply what shall we do tomorrow, but rather what shall we do today in order to get ready for tomorrow."
– Peter Drucker

HAVE YOU PASSED your "best by" date? Are you out of tune and out of touch? To find out, you might take this test. Google "current buzzwords." Do today's vocabulary words, colloquialisms, and slang have relevance to you? Are you conversant with today's technology and tuned in to the latest social media craze? Who currently dominates the air waves, stars in the most popular television series, and brings in the big box-office bucks?

While it's not essential, in most professions, to pass a pop-culture quiz to establish expertise in your chosen field, you must pass today's "currency" test as it applies to what you do. In my field, party and event rental, I must: know the Pantone color of the year; be conversant with what's trending on Pinterest; understand the terms "boho" and "steampunk"; recognize, among others, the names David Tutera, Preston Bailey, and Jennifer Gilbert.

Gilbert is a highly successful female entrepreneur who built a 30 million dollar business, Save the Date, in the event planning space. Along the way she authored the book I Never Promised You a Goodie Bag: A Memoir of a Life Through Events – the Ones You Plan and the Ones You Don't. This work is a must read for anyone in my industry! What book or blog or webcast or TED Talk or conference or other resource can help you stay current in your field?

I suggest there are three primary ways of staying current in what you do. First, join your industry's professional trade organization. In the context of party and event rental, the leading professional trade group most directly related to our industry is the American Rental Association.

ARA has an annual trade show that we've attended each year since our company's formation. ARA publishes Rental Management Magazine, a periodical featuring the latest party and event rental products and services. ARA membership provides a plethora of ancillary benefits as well, including member insurance and credit card processing. Like most trade associations, ARA also supports desirable political outcomes (through a dedicated political action committee) that directly and positively affect rental businesses and rental operations.

Most likely, your industry has a similar group. Get involved and stay involved. Contribute your time and talents to stimulate organizational growth (there's power in numbers) and improve member benefits. Support the group or association, and the people within it, who work hard on your behalf, and on behalf of your industry. Remember, a rising tide lifts all boats, and when your industry prospers, you and your company prosper as well.

Second, ferret out best practices in your industry and adapt to or adopt them. Learn everything you can from anyone who is willing to help you do a better job. Read the books written by experts in your field. Read the magazines, journals and publications written by those who are on the cutting edge in your area of endeavor. When some "big name" in your game makes an appearance in your area, go hear them. Visit and analyze successful operations outside your market (with whom you do not directly compete). When a new superstar in your field appears on the horizon, approach them. Find out what they're doing better or differently.

Third, be an idea magnet. Poll the people. All of us, collectively, know more than any of us individually. Ask your colleagues, in your field or related fields, what's working for them. Find out what they've tried that didn't yield the desired result. And never forget that your home team sometimes knows best. They're uniquely in touch with your market, your customers, and your operation. Listen, especially to the young. They don't know what can't be done . . . and just might be the ones to help you do it.

Relevance in your chosen field is a key ingredient in establishing expertise. Do your views matter to anyone outside your own organization? When you speak about key industry topics, do people listen? They do if you're a recognized expert!

Here are three key ways that I've found to help establish relevance in my bailiwick, and I believe they will work for you. First, avail yourself of every meaningful volunteer role and accept every possible leadership opportunity. Without jeopardizing your business or family relationships, just say "yes." When you're asked to serve on a board or be an officer in an organization that interests you or relates to your industry, step up. Make positive contributions to the organizations in which you're involved. Do what you say you'll do   ... make friends and establish acquaintances ... acquit yourself with grace and dignity. Over time, you'll earn the respect and admiration of your peers and the regard of your competitors.

If you doubt the efficacy of this approach, check my LinkedIn profile. My friends, colleagues, and associates have endorsed my expertise. I'm grateful to each and all who have taken the time to speak well of me and of Premiere.

Second, write and speak well. Write articles or columns for your trade journal or publication. Write blog posts or contribute to an electronic newsletter. Write for your company and your team. Send copies of articles you've written to your clients and customers. If your writings are informative and helpful, you'll soon begin to be regarded as an expert in your field.

Once you write well, learn the art of public speaking. The single most reported fear isn't spiders or heights or alien invasion; it's public speaking. Engage in deliberate practice until you're an accomplished speaker. When the opportunity is presented, agree to address a Rotary Club meeting or be part of a panel discussion. When you've earned a special award or received special recognition, deliver an inspiring acceptance speech. Effective public speaking helps reinforce the perception that you're an accomplished, expert professional.

Finally, be helpful. With the possible exception of aiding and abetting direct competitors, graciously share your knowledge and expertise. When Premiere chose the party and event rental path, we had no rental knowledge or events experience. Thankfully, ours is a generous industry. Early on, we were educated by ARA members who taught industry seminars, served on industry panels, and shared best practices. These industry experts invited us to their stores and allowed us to observe their operations. They shortened our learning curve and saved us countless harsh lessons. We didn't have to repeat the mistakes from which others had already learned. As time has passed, it's been our very great pleasure to return the favor and pay it forward.

Connect with Other Professionals

"Your network is your net worth."
– Porter Gale

"My Golden Rule of Networking is simple:
Don't keep score."
– Harvey Mackay

"You can have everything in life you want if you will just help enough other people get what they want."
– Zig Ziglar

NETWORKING IS DEFINED, in part, as interacting with other people to exchange information and develop contacts, especially to further one's career. Building a network of like-minded industry professionals and taking a leadership role within your (formal or informal) networking group(s) helps to establish and consistently reinforce your expertise.

In the events industry, The National Association for Catering and Events (NACE) and the International Live Events Association (ILEA) are large trade associations with active chapters and thousands of members spread over the globe. Formal networking groups also include a host of small local, state, and national wedding and events industry organizations. Premiere Events is and/or has been an active member of these leading events industry organizations. I have served as president of the Austin ILEA Chapter and spent several years on the NACE-Austin board. Other Premiere team members hold or have held key roles in and have been recognized by our local NACE and ILEA chapters as well.

Why is Premiere so heavily invested in NACE, ILEA, and other lesser-known organizations? Why do we regularly contribute, in cash and in-kind, to organizational activities? What's in it for us?

Professionals in virtually every field of endeavor benefit from active participation in a networking community. Through common experience and shared interests, network members blend their talents and pool their expertise. The exchange of ideas, sharing of leads, and practice of reciprocal referrals enhances products, improves services, and provides increased client and customer value. In our experience and in networking lore, positive connections in a professional community accelerate growth, increase revenues, maximize profits, and stimulate success.

Knowing others in your field, and being known by them, is essential to perceived expertise. What others think and say about you—the opinions they hold and express—is critical to creating a positive mental image in the minds of prospective clients and customers. If a prospective client or customer looks you up online, what will they find? Connect with other professionals. Demonstrate your expertise. Generously share your knowledge and experience. Be involved, engaged, and helpful. Zealously guard your reputation, both online and off!

Personal Success Strategies for Building and Establishing Expertise

"An investment in knowledge pays the best interest."
– Benjamin Franklin

1. Who has most heavily influenced my attitude toward work and achievement?

Have my role models in this context had a positive or negative impact on my performance and success? Can I identify other groups or individuals that might help me build expertise in these areas of my life?

2. Who has had the greatest influence on me in terms of financial matters (e.g. spending, investing, saving)? Do my financial counselors and consultants, formal or informal, help move me closer to, or further from my financial goals? How could other people or groups improve my financial well-being?

3. On a scale of 10 to 1, with 10 being a very good, positive influence and 1 being a very bad, negative influence, how would I rate my influence on those around me? _____ What can I do to improve my influence profile? How might I become a better network builder among coworkers, associates, customers, industry contacts, and others within my orbit?

4. With 10 being a highly regarded expert and 1 being inept and un-skilled, to what extent do I believe others regard me as an expert in my field of endeavor? _____ What specific steps can I take (returning to school, taking continuing education courses, reading and studying the work of experts in my field, writing articles for trade or other magazines, accepting speaking opportunities, etc.) to further develop, and then to establish my expertise?

5. In what specific setting or in what deliberate ways can I practice the skills that are critical to success in my work or business environment?

6. Might there be a mentor or trusted advisor who could help me per-fect my practice techniques (and if so, who might be willing to help?).

7. What professional trade group, association, or organization could help me stay current on the latest industry trends and conversant with the hot topics pertinent to my work or business?

How can I become more involved with the groups, associations, or organizations that matter to me professionally?

8. Who can I include as "human capital" in my idea bank? Who among my coworkers, team members, associates, acquaintances, and others with whom I have (or can make) contact can help me stay relevant and informed, and how will I recruit them?

9. Who in my circle or sphere of influence could benefit from my expertise? How can I share my knowledge, skills, or insights in meaningful and helpful ways?

And Remember . . .

"Networking is not about just connecting people. It's about connecting people with people, people with ideas, and people with opportunities."
– Michele Jennae

"The single greatest 'people skill' is a highly developed and authentic interest in the other person."
– Bob Burg

Chapter 7

The Third "E" = Emotion

"Never be ashamed of what you feel.
You have the right to feel any emotion you want, and
to do what makes you happy. That's my life motto."
– Demi Lovato

"Your intellect may be confused, but your emotions
will never lie to you."
– Roger Ebert

PSYCHOLOGISTS AND OTHER social scientists have studied "emotion" since the term first came into use in the late 16th century. Derived from a French word for "stir up" and a Latin word for "move out, remove or agitate," the word "emotion" was first used synonymously with "strong feeling" in the 1650s. The term came to describe any feeling in the early 1800's.

And for the past 300 years, psychologists and other social scientists have posited, proffered, and proposed a myriad of definitions for the term. While the scientific meaning varies from researcher to researcher and field to field, in everyday speech, emotion has come to mean "any relatively brief conscious experience characterized by intense mental activity and a high degree of pleasure or displeasure."

Managing emotion, the subject of this chapter, is an important part of a successful-living strategy. Our work on the "third E" will not focus on the scientific aspects of intense mental activity. Although current research and writings on this topic are both fascinating and enlightening, our focus will be on emotion's practical implications. We won't spend time here debating the "why" of what we're feeling but focusing on the "what" to do about it. We'll be more intent on being more intentional about channeling emotions and utilizing emotional energy in ways that enhance our chances of being successful, by our own previously established definitions, and living well.

Afraid of Feeling?

"To give vent now and then to his feelings, whether of pleasure or discontent, is a great ease to a man's heart."
– Francesco Guicciardini

"We all know that being able to express deep emotion can literally save a person's life, and suppressing emotion can kill you — both spiritually and physically."
– Lisa Kleypas

I'M NOT AFRAID of heights . . . just of falling. I love a spectacular view from the top. Gazing down from a precipice is exhilarating and inspiring when there's no real risk involved. That's why millions of people each year view Paris from the Eiffel Tower or gaze down at the city of Chicago from the glassed-in top floor of the Sears Tower or take in the Big Apple from the top of Lady Liberty. There's virtually NO RISK associated with making it to the top of these iconic landmarks. A stunning vantage point can be easily achieved with virtually no down side. Each of these attractions has a handy elevator that painlessly and pleasantly whisks you to your destination.

Contrast these all but effortless adventures with an ascent of Mount Everest. As of 2018, 5,294 humans had reached the Everest summit (although the mountain has been summited 9,159 times). The average Everest climb takes about two months and, according to Alan Narnette (http://www.alanarnette.com/blog/2019/12/01/how-much-does-it-cost-to-climb-mount-everest-2020-edition/) is an expensive proposition. "So, how much does it cost to climb Mount Everest?" Narnette's blog advises "As I've said for years, the short answer is a car or at least $30,000, but most people pay about $45,000, and some will pay as much as $160,000! Climbing Everest is arduous, dangerous, risky, physically challenging, unpleasant, demanding, and even deadly. Yet people are flocking to Nepal in record numbers to take up the Everest challenge.

Fear of feeling is, in many ways, akin to fear of falling. What would you attempt if you knew you couldn't fall? What would you feel if you knew you couldn't be hurt? If acknowledging and embracing your emotions required little effort, minimal investment, and almost no risk, how would that change your perspective about exploring relationships, establishing friendships, supporting charitable organizations, or lending a helping hand?

How would your new-found emotional courage manifest itself? Would you foster a child, adopt a shelter animal, visit your ailing grandmother, or reach out to a friend going through tough times? If you knew that the potential emotional gain would outweigh the possible emotional pain, would you take a chance on a budding romance? Perhaps you would be brave enough for parenthood (of two-or four-legged babies), strong enough to love your team, caring enough to do right by your customers, secure enough to respect your competitors, and compassionate enough to donate (your time, energy, or money) to a cause that resonates with you.

The many health benefits of positive emotions are well documented. Some longevity studies suggest that happily married couples live longer, healthier lives than their single counterparts. While marriage, or robust and emotionally intimate relationships outside of marriage, guarantees neither happiness nor longevity, there can be little argument that loving, mutually supportive relationships enrich our lives in many meaningful ways.

According to a Mayo Clinic online resource, friendship provides a myriad of benefits as well. "Friends can help you celebrate good times and provide support during bad times. Friends prevent loneliness and give you a chance to offer needed companionship, too. Friends can also: increase your sense of belonging and purpose; boost your happiness and reduce your stress; improve your self-confidence and self-worth; help you cope with traumas, such as divorce, serious illness, job loss or the death of a loved one, and encourage you to change or avoid unhealthy lifestyle habits. Friends play a significant role in promoting overall health. Adults with strong social support have a reduced risk of depression, high blood pressure and an unhealthy body mass index (BMI). Studies have even found that older adults with a rich social life are likely to live longer than their peers."

Let go of the fear of feeling and embrace the exhilaration of the amazing life view that can be yours "for a song." It might not be as easy as an elevator ride, but it's not as brutal as an Everest climb, either. Google "positive emotions" and almost every list will include love, compassion, caring, and kindness. Combine these feelings with joy, gratitude, cheerfulness, and hope, then mix well. You'll have a powerful recipe for emotional success. You really can come out ahead by following your feelings.

Keep Your Balance

> "Just as your car runs more smoothly and
> requires less energy to go faster and farther when the
> wheels are in perfect alignment, you perform better
> when your thoughts, feelings, emotions, goals and
> values are in balance."
> – Brian Tracy

> "Feelings are much like waves, we can't stop them from
> coming but we can choose which ones to surf."
> – Jonathan Martensson

ACHIEVING A SMOOTH highway ride requires that our tires be properly balanced. The better our wheels are aligned, the more pleasant the drive. Our vehicles are easier to steer and require less effort to control when good balance and proper alignment are established and maintained. Earlier in this book, we described how simple, easy, and affordable it is to achieve well-balanced, properly aligned wheels. Achieving emotional balance takes considerably more effort.

When our emotions are out of balance, when there's a surplus of fear or an exaggerated sense of euphoria in our lives, our relationships, and our work can be difficult to manage. It's the link between feelings and actions that compels us to seek emotional balance.

For purposes of this discussion, let's define emotional balance as the state of contentment achieved when negative emotions (fear, self-doubt, despair, rage, and the like) are explored, addressed, and exorcised and positive emotions (joy, love, hope, gratitude, kindness, and kindred feelings) are consciously and deliberately embraced.

Scientists speculate that genetics are responsible for about 50% of our emotional content—but the other half of how we feel and what we do with those feelings is up to us. Failure to find our emotional sweet spot, whether we're tilting, emotionally, in a negative or positive direction, still leaves us teetering on the edge and in danger of falling. Righting ourselves, emotionally speaking, enables us to be our best self, allows us to know true joy, renders us more effective at work and at home, and increases our capacity to love and help others.

Achieving emotional balance requires the ability to engage in the healthy practices of reflection and introspection but do so without self-absorption. Knowing what we're feeling, naming our emotions, and identifying our feelings correctly are the first steps in achieving the balance we seek. "I'm so mad," "I'm really sad," "I'm so glad," "I'm truly grateful." Mad, Sad, Grateful, Glad . . . we must know what we're feeling and give it an accurate name before we can know why or how to "feel better".

Once we know what, we can begin to ask why. An inner reflective dialogue or introspective self-conversation regarding feelings of anger, for example, might go something like this. "Why am I feeling so angry? Was it something I did (or maybe didn't do) or something that was done to me? I think I'm angry because John was really rude to me today in our team meeting. It made me feel bad when he called me out in front of my coworkers. If he's got a beef with me (or my sales figures or my handling of a situation or whatever), he should come to me personally and discuss it privately."

How can we restore our emotional balance in this, or in any "he did or said this to me" or "she did or said that" situation? We know we cannot control the actions or thoughts of others. All we can control is our own response to another's behavior, whether we perceive that behavior as objectionable, threatening, and unkind or loving, helpful, and gracious.

Exploring why we feel this way or that way and ascertaining whether those feelings are healthy, justified, and appropriate is a start. Discovering whether our emotions make us feel better or worse, and in turn, act better or worse, is progress. Determining whether we've acted in some way that contributed to or escalated the situation allows us to consider alternative responses that might have enabled us to handle a situation differently or that might work better for us the next time. These are the important inner reflective questions we might be asking or introspective dialogue we could be having.

And these inner reflective questions and introspective internal dialogue lead us to informed conclusions. Those conclusions, if they're to be helpful in restoring our emotional balance, must lead to positive actions. The conclusion and the follow-up action in the "John" example might go something like this.

"I really can't afford to be angry with John nor have him angry with me. These angry feelings impair my effectiveness at work and may drive a wedge between me and the team. When I take these angry feelings home, they make me edgy and short-tempered. No good can come of this! So, first, I'm going to talk to John and apologize for . . ." (being late with that assignment or making a mistake in handling an order or failing to make an expected sale – or for whatever is the source of conflict). "Then I'm also going to do better by" . . . (list specific actions to take, future behaviors to exhibit that will improve performance, alternative responses to test that may de-escalate or resolve the conflict more appropriately and positively). "I'm also going to talk to John about coming to me, personally and privately, when there's an issue or problem, so that I might have an opportunity to remedy the situation and improve my results. Past that, and doing my very best, I'm going to let this go. I'll achieve better results at work, restore John's confidence in me, and relieve my family of the burden of my anger."

The approach outlined in this section, inner reflective questions and introspective internal dialogue, is certainly not new or original. Some people struggle to gain insight without assistance and support. A trusted friend or family member, a minister or other person of faith, or, when needed, a professional therapist can help and guide us in gaining insight into our feelings. Self-help experts recommend a variety of beneficial, healing DIY emotional-balance therapies, including meditation, breathing exercises, yoga (and other forms of physical activity), and relaxation (including daydreaming, listening to music, and spa treatments—my personal favorite).

Regardless of the remedy you choose or the emotion with which you're dealing, a feeling that significantly upsets your emotional balance must be addressed. Like a cancer or an infection, an untreated out-of-balance emotional state rarely gets better on its own. Don't let an unwelcome emotion fester and poison your life. Deal with it, and restore emotional balance. Maintain a healthy state of emotional contentment!

Emotional Intelligence

"If your emotional abilities aren't in hand, if you don't have self-awareness, if you are not able to manage your distressing emotions, if you can't have empathy and have effective relationships, then no matter how smart you are, you are not going to get very far."
– Daniel Goleman

DANIEL GOLEMAN POPULARIZED the term "Emotional Intelligence" (EI) in 1995, when his book bearing that title was published. Wikipedia reports that Goleman's conclusions about the importance of EI and its relative contribution to successful living may have been overstated, but few psychologists or social scientists would argue that understanding and managing our own emotions isn't healthier and more desirable than the alternative. Further, awareness of the emotions of others, and the use of that awareness to moderate our attitudes and behavior toward them, is clearly a factor in building and nurturing healthy and successful relationships. And successful relationships with family, friends, colleagues and others significantly contribute to living a successful life.

Travis Bradberry, writing for inc.com, says this "When emotional intelligence (EQ) first appeared to the masses, it served as the missing link in a peculiar finding: people with average IQs outperform those with the highest IQs 70 percent of the time. Decades of research now point to emotional intelligence as being the critical factor that sets star performers apart from the rest of the pack. The connection is so strong that 90 percent of top performers have high emotional intelligence. Emotional intelligence is the 'something' in each of us that is a bit intangible. It affects how we manage behavior, navigate social complexities, and make personal decisions to achieve positive results."

Bradberry's article (inc.com/travis-bradberry/are-you-emotionally-intelligent-here-s-how-to-know-for-sure.html) goes on to list eighteen aspects of emotional intelligence. Psychologists and social scientists generally agree that emotional intelligence is a learned behavior and further, that any and all of us can increase our emotional intelligence at any time and throughout our lives. The eighteen aspects offered by Bradberry suggest eighteen building blocks for gaining control of our emotional lives and for relating to others on a deeper, more meaningful, more successful level. You may wish to read them for yourself.

A related entrepreneur.com article offers ten behaviors "that are the hallmarks of a low EQ." These are the behaviors you want to eliminate from your repertoire. "1. You get stressed easily. 2. You have difficulty asserting yourself. 3. You have a limited emotional vocabulary. 4. You make assumptions quickly and defend them vehemently. 5. You hold grudges. 6. You don't let go of mistakes. 7. You often feel misunderstood. 8. You don't know your triggers. 9. You don't get angry. 10. You blame other people for how they make you feel."

Inc.com (Justin-Bariso/how-can-i-build-emotional-intelligence) suggests these seven steps for learning how to "make emotions work for you, instead of against you. It all begins," says Bariso, "with focusing on your thoughts. The key," he continues, "is to control the reactions to your feelings—to make sure you're acting in a way that you won't later regret." The article continues with an analysis of the emotional skills (self-awareness, self-regulation, and motivation) that we need to manage ourselves and those we need to manage our relationships with others (empathy and social skills).

There are a myriad of other online resources dealing with this topic, and I encourage you to explore them. There are online EQ (or EI) tests, online strategies for strengthening your EQ, online guides for "exercising" your emotional self-management and others-focused emotional muscles.

Who among us, with a readily available, easily accessible EQ-building toolbox just a mouse click away, would think or say, "Nah, I'm good? Sure, I get stressed out and worked up. Yeah, I might take my frustrations out on my" . . . spouse, kids, coworkers, whomever or whatever – you fill in the blank, "but that's just how I am." Which of us, now fully aware that EQ is a significant factor in determining our individual emotional well-being and the health of our relationships with others, would rationally and reasonably fail to take full advantage of the plethora of options available for boosting our EQ?

You're not that person. You're not content with anything less than your emotional best. Now, knowing that you have the capacity, you can expand your emotional horizons. You can make a lifelong commitment to better understanding and managing your emotional self. You can recognize the importance of achieving and maintaining emotional balance . . . at home, at work and even at play. Become excited about using your EQ to make the most of every relationship investment, and act on that excitement.

Regardless of your current EQ, you can become emotionally smarter. You can become an improved version of your emotional self – gain greater self-control and a heightened sense of emotional fulfillment. You can become a more caring and emotionally connected partner, a more conscious and emotionally present parent, a more tolerant and caring friend. Today is the day to begin your journey of emotional self-discovery. There's nothing to be gained by waiting!

Personal Success Strategies for Emotional Intelligence Improvement

"Emotional intelligence is a way of recognizing, understanding, and choosing how we think, feel, and act. It shapes our interactions with others and our understanding of ourselves. It defines how and what we learn; it allows us to set priorities; it determines the majority of our daily actions. Research suggests it is responsible for as much as 80 percent of the "success" in our lives."
– J. Freedman

"Emotional intelligence is the ability to sense, understand, and effectively apply the power and acumen of emotions as a source of human energy, information, connection, and influence."
– Robert K. Cooper, PhD

1. Thinking of my typical day at work, what three positive emotions do I experience most often?

What one happy emotion is most important to me in the workplace, and when, specifically, have I capitalized on that emotion to achieve some positive outcome?

2. On the flip side, what three negative emotions do I most commonly experience in the workplace?

Choosing one negative emotion from my list, how, specifically, has that emotion impacted me negatively in my job?

3. How, specifically, can I cultivate attitudes and behaviors that result in more fulfilling, rewarding, enjoyable, and emotionally positive work experiences?

"75 percent of careers are derailed for reasons related to emotional competencies, including inability to handle interpersonal problems; unsatisfactory team leadership during times of difficulty or conflict; or inability to adapt to change or elicit trust."
– Center for Creative Leadership

4. Perhaps it's honing listening skills, or feeling and expressing empathy, or taking an online EQ test to identify current emotional functioning. Maybe it's making time for Inner Reflective Questioning and Introspective Internal Dialogue. Whatever "it" is, what will I do, before this month ends, to raise my EQ?

5. What specific actions, be it a book (or books) I'll read, a course I'll take, a candid conversation I'll initiate, a behavior I'll practice until it becomes a habit—what specific steps will I take to have an improved EQ before this year ends?

6. How can I think my way into a new way of acting or act my way into a new way of thinking that either helps me cope with emotional negatives in the workplace or reduces the frequency of emotionally negative situations?

"When dealing with people, remember you are not dealing with creatures of logic, but with creatures of emotion."
– Dale Carnegie

"Too often we underestimate the power of a touch, a smile, a kind word, a listening ear, an honest compliment, or the smallest act of caring, all of which have the potential to turn a life around."
– Leo Buscaglia

7. Thinking of my typical day at home, what three positive emotions do I experience most often?

Choosing the one happy emotion that's most important to me in my home life, I can describe a time when I capitalized on that emotion to achieve some positive outcome for myself or to help another. How did I constructively use this emotion?

8. What three negative emotions do I most often experience at home?

Choosing one negative emotion from my list, I can describe how that emotion causes issues for me or creates problems for my family. What is the negative emotion, and how does it adversely impact me or the people I care about? What can I do to help alleviate the stress and avoid the hurt my negative emotions may be causing?

9. How can I cultivate the attitudes and behaviors that result in a more fulfilling, rewarding, enjoyable, and emotionally positive home life?

10. What specific actions, be it a book (or books) I'll read, an event (retreat, marriage encounter, church conference, etc.) I'll attend, a candid conversation I'll initiate, a behavior I'll practice until it becomes a habit...what specific steps will I take to have greater positive emotional energy in my home?

11. How can I think my way into a new way of acting or act my way into a new way of thinking that either helps me cope with emotional negatives at home or reduces the frequency of emotionally negative outcomes for me and those I love?

Chapter 8

The "Z" = Zeal

"Experience shows that success is due
less to ability than to zeal."
– Charles Buxton

"Zeal will do more than knowledge."
– William Hazlitt

IF EVER A beautiful, powerful, positive word has been abused, misapplied, and improperly used, that word is Zeal. While we could have made the final letter in our Simple Success Strategies an "E" for Enthusiasm, we wouldn't have spelled anything but PPPEEE. That final E seemed out of place for me, and since Zeal and Enthusiasm have essentially the same meaning and can, in fact, be used interchangeably, we'll switch back and forth between the two words in this chapter—and end our Simple Strategies initialization well, I think, with the letter Z for Zeal.

Zeal is defined as "great energy or enthusiasm in pursuit of a cause or objective." No trait, quality, or characteristic in our Simple Strategies Success formula is more important than zeal or enthusiasm. Winston Churchill defined success as "going from failure to failure without losing enthusiasm." No matter how Positive you are, how Persistent, how Principled, how Energetic—regardless of the Expertise you attain or the Emotional Mastery you demonstrate, Zeal helps you press on. Zeal and enthusiasm help you battle discouragement and overcome disappointment.

Absent zeal, problems become obstacles, and obstacles morph into stumbling blocks that impede our progress and block our path. Without enthusiasm we may falter, becoming disillusioned, disheartened, disinterested. When there's no real zeal for life and living, no passion for what we're doing or what we're planning to do or for the people with whom we're making our life journey, nothing else really matters. Nothing at all.

That's a dangerous place to be . . . the place where darkness and despair lurk in the shadows, where the light of positivity and the energy of passion can be snuffed out by doubt and fear. Don't go there! And if you find yourself there, don't stay there. And if you can't find your way back on your own, if you can't summon the energy or enthusiasm to work your way out—get help. Recapture your joie de vivre—your exuberant enjoyment of life. Live enthusiastically. Be zealous for joyful, successful living.

Heed these wise words from Martha Beck. "When fear makes your choices for you, no security measures on earth will keep the things you dread from finding you. But if you can avoid avoidance—if you can choose to embrace experiences out of passion, enthusiasm, and a readiness to feel whatever arises—then nothing, nothing in all this dangerous world, can keep you from being safe." Be zealous, both in overcoming your fears and doubts and in treasuring all the good that comes your way.

Nothing Great . . .

"Nothing great was ever achieved without enthusiasm."
–Ralph Waldo Emerson

"The real secret of success is enthusiasm."
– Walter Chrysler

"There is a real magic in enthusiasm. It spells the difference between mediocrity and accomplishment."
– Norman Vincent Peale

EARTH-SHAKING ACCOMPLISHMENTS require unwavering enthusiasm. Life-altering achievements find their seed in the zeal to better humankind or to be the first or to be the best—the wealthiest or even the most powerful. They grow in the fertile soil of passion and persistence. They thrive in the sunlight of positive energy. They wither in an atmosphere of self-doubt and will die just as surely as a tender plant placed in the dark or left out in the cold.

Orison Swett Marden said this: "Nearly all the great improvements, discoveries, inventions, and achievements which have elevated and blessed humanity have been the triumphs of enthusiasm." History tells us about brave and pioneering men and women who had a dream, and who pursued that dream with a zealous fervor. Pick up a copy of Inc. or Forbes or Fortune, or books written by or about successful men and women. You'll find that extraordinarily successful people are on fire with enthusiasm for what they do. That zeal—that fervor—that enthusiasm—that passion burns so bright that others cannot help but notice—and noticing, are inexorably attracted, like metal to a magnet or a moth to the flame. Nothing is more appealing and attractive than that glowing aura of success.

When zeal for a cause or a brand or a dream or a hope meets accomplishment, it's the perfect storm. Perhaps Samuel Taylor Coleridge said it best. "Nothing is so contagious as enthusiasm." Every team sport bears witness to this adage. Even the brightest coaches and most talented players can snatch defeat from the jaws of victory when the opponent displays greater passion and enthusiasm. Home field advantage isn't about a field or a stadium; it's about absorbing energy from the fans and feeding off their passion for "The W" —their zeal for making the playoffs or winning the big one.

And no Olympic athlete, golfer, tennis player, or professional bull rider ever won the gold medal, green jacket, US Open Trophy, or shiny buckle without passion. When the fire of passion is extinguished and the love of the game dies, all the experience, skill, and ability in the world won't be enough to preserve the winning streak. You've seen the upsets—the number-one ranked participant in any given sport on any given day "zones out" and is defeated by a less talented but more determined, zealous opponent. Fueled by passion and filled with enthusiasm from early successes in the battle, the less expert competitor prevails.

Hence the ancient exhortation generally attributed to Confucius: "Choose a job you love, and you'll never have to work a day in your life." I would add this corollary: "Choose to love the job that you do. Embrace your labors with passion and enthusiasm. Be zealous in your work, and enjoy every day in your life."

Confucius also said, "When you are laboring for others, let it be with the same zeal as if it were for yourself." Make that conscious choice, and you cannot help but succeed in your work, whatever the endeavor. Further, you'll always be your own boss, because you'll be in charge of you. You, and only you, can determine the quality of your output and the character of your contributions. You, and only you, can decide whether you'll be a committed, conscientious team player or a coasting, cynical underachiever.

Sure, someone else may have the power to give you an assignment or ask you to complete a task. But you have the power to make every project a challenge you gladly accept. Every task can become a test to which you zealously give your highest and best effort, determined to continuously expand your knowledge and improve your performance. You may have an employer – or you may be an employer – in either case, you work for your team and for your customers – and ultimately, you work for you. Do your work with enthusiasm.

Zealously, Not Jealously

"The surest route to breeding jealousy is to compare. Since jealousy comes from feeling less than another, comparisons only fan the fires."
– Dorothy Corkille Briggs

"A competent and self-confident person is incapable of jealousy in anything. Jealousy is invariably a symptom of neurotic insecurity."
– Robert A. Heinlein

"The jealous are troublesome to others, but a torment to themselves."
– William Penn

A REFERENCE TO the text of Desiderata was included in our first "P" (for Positivity) Chapter. There's great advice throughout that work, but the phrase, "If you compare yourself with others, you may become vain and bitter; for always there will be greater and lesser persons than yourself," is of particular relevance as a successful living strategy. Some people seem to have it all: wealthy parents, a privileged upbringing, good looks, an Ivy-League education. They have everything money can buy—and much of what it can't. They have a loving spouse (or significant other) and beautiful (mostly well-behaved) children. Even their pets are precious! They have a wide circle of friends and acquaintances. They enjoy the respect of their peers and the adoration of strangers.

But all these advantages aren't an automatic ticket to a happy life or successful living. If they were, absent the "loving spouse," Princess Diana certainly "had it all." Google "What made Princess Diana Unhappy?" and you'll find one author's perspective. In Chapter One of her book, Diana in Search of Herself, Portrait of a Troubled Princess, Sally Bedell Smith offers the following insights.

"'The world probably would have heard little of Diana Spencer had she not married the Prince of Wales. She would either have been a countrywoman, just like her sisters, and dissolved into the atmosphere,' said a male friend who knew her from her teenage years, 'or she would have married an achiever who offered more of a challenge but would have gone off and had an affair, and she would have divorced the husband in short order.'"

"Diana lived only thirty-six years, all of them amid privilege and wealth: the first half in the rarefied cocoon of the British upper class, the second in the highly visible bubble of royal protocol and pageantry. Her married life was unnatural by any measure—'bizarre' her brother Charles, Earl Spencer, called it in his eulogy of Diana. Much of her royal existence was lonely and regimented, but tabloid headlines invested its large and small events with high drama."

"But in the solitude of her apartment at Kensington Palace, the engaging public Diana often descended into a lonely, adolescent solipsism" [extreme preoccupation with and indulgence of one's feelings, desires, etc.; egoistic self-absorption]. "'The time spent alone reviewing every situation and having no friends was for planning and plotting,' said Haslam. 'Diana would dwell on her perceived inadequacies, ponder the betrayals of her past and present, and think obsessively about her enemies, both real and imagined. Her thoughts would plunge her into tears and sometimes vengeful schemes. At such moments, she made her worst decisions.'"

Diana's story, her roller-coaster life and tragic death, vividly illustrate many of the points made throughout this book, perhaps none more poignantly than William Penn's words, repeated here for emphasis. "The jealous are troublesome to others, but a torment to themselves." Despite living every young girl's "princess" fantasy, Diana led an often troubled and unhappy adult life. Was jealousy at the root of her troubles?

It's a complex question with no definitive answer (since only Diana herself could know the source of her insecurities), but perhaps, in comparing herself to others, Princess Diana may have focused on what she lacked rather than what she had. Maybe she lamented having married a man who openly preferred another woman. She might have envied others their intellect and education, since, according to Smith's book (previously referenced), "She frequently belittled her intelligence, saying she was 'thick as a plank' or had a brain 'the size of a pea.'"

Whatever it was that plagued this princess, she could, at any time, have chosen a different path. She could have elected to focus on the positives in her life and to better cope with her challenges. She could have capitalized, to an even greater degree, on her unique gifts and astounding popularity, leveraging those advantages to zealously champion and support many charitable causes and humanitarian efforts. She could have "found herself," and loved herself, as a mother to her sons, as the embodiment of grace and charm, and as a gracious and generous role model—all of which, for the most part, she was. She could have worried less about the opinions and judgments of others and cared only that she succeed on her own terms and by her own definition.

Ryan Holiday ends his 2016 book, Ego is the Enemy, with these words: "I want to conclude this book with the idea . . . that it's admirable to want to be better businessmen or businesswomen, better athletes, better competitors. We should want to be better informed, better off financially . . . we should want . . . to do great things. But no less impressive an accomplishment: being better people, being happier people, being balanced people, being content people, being humble and selfless people."

"What is left? asks Holiday. "Your choices," he answers. "What will you do with this information? Not just now, but going forward?"

What will you learn, I ask, from the story of Diana—and of countless other figures throughout ancient history and modern times? How will you be affected by the stories of those who seemingly had it all—yet for one reason or another, couldn't be happy—couldn't sustain the effort or maintain their enthusiasm. Many tragic figures didn't simply walk away or quit while ahead or go gently into that good night. They spiraled downward, becoming their own worst enemies. Despite all they had and all that they'd done, they allowed jealousy, insecurity, and ego to rob them of joy, and sometimes, in the extreme, of life itself.

Don't take that path—don't make comparisons! Keep your eye on the prize—your prize. Focus on what you have, not what you lack. Nothing anyone else has and nothing that someone else enjoys takes away from you. Adopt an attitude of gratitude. Be zealous—not jealous.

How Badly do YOU Want It?

"Ambition is so powerful a passion in the human breast, that however high we reach we are never satisfied."
– Henry Wadsworth Longfellow

"Character cannot be developed in ease and quiet. Only through experience of trial and suffering can the soul be strengthened, ambition inspired and success achieved."
– Helen Keller

"Ambition is important. Of course you can't get anywhere without talent, but there are a lot of talented people. To succeed, you have to be the most ambitious talented person."
– Natalie Massenet

RESEARCH NATALIE MASSENET online, as I did, and read her story. Massenet is a financial success. The fashion merchandising company she founded, Net-A-Porter (later acquired by and merged with a competitor) was innovative, creative, and cutting-edge. Massenet, according to Wikipedia, "changed the way designer fashion is retailed." She has been described as "fashion's favourite fashion success story." Massenet's accomplishments demonstrate her assertion that "to succeed you have to be the most ambitious talented person."

Was Tiger Woods the most talented golfer of his day . . . or the most ambitious talented golfer? Was Michael Jordan the most talented basketball player of his time . . . or the most ambitious talented basketball player? Is Tom Brady the most talented football quarterback ever (with more game wins and the most Super Bowl wins in history) . . . or the most ambitious talented football player?

Ryan Holiday (previously quoted), Austin, Texas, author and entrepreneur, is credited with this quote: "Work hard, take it seriously, embrace your ambition." Successful men and women around the globe and in all walks of life embrace their ambition, work hard, and take their work seriously. Whether they're searching for the cure for cancer, formulating innovative investment strategies, planning the next technological breakthrough, or studying for their bar exam, they want "it" very, very badly. They're zealously pursing their ambition—they're driven and passionate and persistent.

What goal or dream do you care about so much that you'll do "whatever it takes" (without compromising your principles or at the expense of others) to achieve it? What job or position or financial pinnacle or life situation do you want so badly that you'll make "it" the focus of your energies and endeavors? What is so important to you that it's your first conscious thought in the morning and your last conscious thought at night? How badly do you want "it"?

This question brings us full circle. In the introduction to this work, we each defined success on our own terms. We articulated a vision of successful living, for ourselves, and if we have them, for our families. Now, this is where push comes to shove—where the rubber meets the road. This is when, even if the going gets tough, the tough get going.

Today, the going is particularly tough. Premiere Events (Austin) and Party Time Rentals (Bryan-College Station, TX), are zealously battling COVID-19 fallout. In early March, 2020, the events world we'd known was plunged into chaos when Austin's South by Southwest (SXSW) was abruptly cancelled. This typically two-week event includes Conferences and Festivals and brings millions of hospitality industry dollars into Austin and surrounding communities. On March 6th, shock waves rocked our industry. Some three weeks later, a Shelter-In-Place order further decimated the hospitality and events industry. Restaurants and bars were closed until further notice. No travel— no hotel stays. Celebrations of every kind, for any reason, were forbidden. No weddings, no funerals. No company conferences, no corporate gatherings. No milestone birthdays, no anniversaries. Nothing.

At first, our hope was for a speedy recovery. Many suggested the virus couldn't survive the Texas heat, and it would all be over come summer. How wrong we were. Our businesses, like many others, were allowed to reopen in May, albeit with a strict pandemic protocol aimed at "protecting", as best we could, both our teams and our customers. Adding insult to injury, event holders who were unable to hold their planned wedding or other celebration during the shutdown wanted a refund of their deposit, and were loath to take no (when offered an indefinite postponement credit) for an answer.

Payroll Protection Plan funds allowed us to retain our staff, and to pay them for "staying home." An Economic Impact Disaster Loan (EIDL) was directed to refunding those customers whose events fell between March 25th and May 4th, the duration of the Texas lockdown. As of this writing, we're operating at less than 50% of what we would be doing in a normal year. To say it's been tough is a gross understatement.

After 19 years of positive revenue growth and a series of impressive "wins", COVID-19 has presented unprecedented challenges. It's taken all that we have to stay the course. We've applied all the PPPEEEZ formula strategies to stay afloat. We're hanging in and hanging on. We've been Persistent, refusing to surrender; actively conveyed positive messages to our team and our customers; worked hard to keep up our Energy. We've honed our Expertise through countless virtual webinars, all while struggling to keep our negative Emotions in check and our positive emotions front and center. We've Zealously pursued every potential pivot and opportunity.

Despite it all, I'm zealously continuing to pursue One Big Thing in the unpredictable life I'm living today. My aim is to continue building a financial legacy, even if that means repurposing our resources and redirecting our energies. We can only wait the hoped-for recovery so long.

In the process, we're striving to set a life example that will benefit our children and their children for generations. My eye is ever on that target. My dream is to see them all be more successful and more joyful than their father/grandfather and I have been.

I'm zealously working to see this book successfully published, and after that, to have it widely read and its lessons applied. My hope is that these words enhance the success, at work and at home, of at least one person who puts in the work and reaps the rewards of the PPPEEEZ strategy. I want to realize my dream and to live the life I've imagined, though it may look somewhat different in the years ahead. And I want to help and support fellow travelers on their success journey as well. Through this book, through my author-page blogs, through my author Facebook page, and in other ways down the road, I want to "be here" for my readers. (You can reach out to me, anytime, at www.delorescrum. com or email me directly at delores@delorescrum.com).

How zealously do you want the successful life you've imagined? Unless you want to succeed, by your own definition, so strongly, so intensely, so passionately that you're fully committed to having it all, you'll never get to where you want to be. You'll never realize your fondest dreams. Unless you want it so badly that you can "taste it," it will elude, tease, and tantalize. If my experience holds true for you, and you look back five, ten, twenty, or fifty years from now, it won't be the things you did that you'll regret, but the things you didn't do. Dare to live the life you deserve!

The life changes you don't make today won't be any easier to make tomorrow. The challenges you reject this week won't look any smaller next week, next month, or next year. Don't spend another day wishing things were better or different, or that you were better or different. Heed the words of Henry David Thoreau, who said: "I learned this, at least, by my experiment: that if one advances confidently in the direction of his dreams, and endeavors to live the life which he has imagined, he will meet with a success unexpected in common hours."

The road to hell is paved with good intentions, so stop "fixing to," quit "meaning to," abandon "getting around to"—as Yoda says, "Do. Or do not. There is no try." Start living your dream today!

Personal Success Strategies for Maximizing Your Enthusiasm and Zealously Pursuing Your Ambitions

"Fires can't be made with dead embers,
nor can enthusiasm be stirred by spiritless men.
Enthusiasm in our daily work lightens effort
and turns even labor into pleasant tasks."
– James A. Baldwin

"Zeal is a volcano, on the peak of which the grass
of indecisiveness does not grow."
– Kahlil Gibran

1. Reflecting on my life, what pursuit, activity, possibility, or dream lights the brightest fire in me?

2. Where does my passion lie, and how have I demonstrated my zeal and enthusiasm for that which excites me?

3. On a scale of 1 (really low) to 10 (amazing!), how enthusiastic am I about the work I do today? _____ What would I like my enthusiasm number to be? _____ How will I achieve that level of zeal? To live more zealously, will I choose a job (or work or hobby) I enjoy or choose to love the job (or work or hobby) that I do?

4. This chapter suggests that I can always be my own boss because "I am in charge of me." Do I accept this assertion and feel empowered by this truth? What will I do better or differently as a result of this realization?

5. Do I autograph my work with excellence? What would it take for me to zealously give my best effort at work, and how would giving my best impact my work experience?

6. Does the story of Princess Diana resonate with me? Do I see a lesson in her struggles, or the related struggle of others that can apply to my life, and if so, what could I learn from her or their experience?

"Ambition leads me not only farther than any other man has been before me, but as far as I think it possible for man to go."
– James Cook

"I've got a great ambition to die of exhaustion rather than boredom."
–Thomas Carlyle

"Our ambition should be to rule ourselves, the true kingdom for each one of us; and true progress is to know more, and be more, and to do more."
– Oscar Wilde

7. What goal or dream do I care about so much that I'll do "whatever it takes" (short of compromising my principles or at the expense of others) to achieve it?

8. How, specifically, will I demonstrate a zealous ambition and unwavering enthusiasm to attain that goal or achieve that dream? What specific actions will I take, and by when, exactly, will I undertake them to move confidently in the direction of my dream?

Final Thoughts

HERE'S A LIST of traits, qualities and characteristics I believe are important to Successful Living, but that didn't fit nicely into our PPPEEEZ categories. Adopt and internalize these attitudes and behaviors, and I believe that you, and those around you, will be the better for it. If we all behaved in these ways, surely the world as we know it would be profoundly and forever changed for the better.

Treat Everyone with Genuine Kindness. Regardless of the relative importance with which you regard another's circumstances in life, the work that they do, or the role that they play, treat everyone you meet and with whom you interact with genuine kindness. There's nothing at all attractive about rude or condescending behavior. Don't be a jerk! It makes you seem small and petty—it makes the people around you uncomfortable. Inconsiderate behavior toward others is an insidious poison that accumulates in your system. It steals your energy and robs you of joy.

Be Polite. Life offers a myriad of opportunities to be polite, kind, and helpful when you're attuned to others and aware of their struggles. Being polite speaks to the quality of your character and the generosity of your spirit.

Play Fair. Whether it's a meaningless game of bridge or a high-stakes poker tournament, always play fair. If you cheat in games, sports, life, or in any context, you rob yourself of the true joy of winning. And you start down a perilous path. Cheating in even the smallest and most inconsequential thing makes cheating at larger and truly meaningful things all the easier. Remember that, ultimately, eventually, virtually every cheater is caught and exposed. That outcome is never, ever pretty.

If It's Not Yours, Don't Keep It. From time to time, you may find something that doesn't belong to you. I have had that experience . . .

and I've also left things that did belong to me in places I shouldn't have. When you find things that belong to others, look for the "person in charge" with whom you could safely leave them. Or look for identifying marks or information that will allow you to return what you've found directly to its rightful owner. When I've lost things, somehow the right person always had them and returned them to me intact. Helping make sure that what you find of value is returned to its rightful owner is the right thing to do. And whether or not the good karma comes back to you, doing the right thing feels good.

Be Prompt. Punctuality shows that you value the time of others and that you can successfully manage your own. Be on time and demonstrate that you're considerate of those to whom you've made a commitment and that they can rely on you. Being late conveys the opposite message. If circumstances beyond your control intervene, immediately alert the person expecting you. Handle the situation professionally and appropriately.

Be Slow to Anger and Quick to Forgive. Most perceived slights or seeming acts of disrespect or inconsideration just aren't worth expending negative emotional energy. Chances are the perpetrator is totally unaware of his or her actions and most likely had no ill intent. That's generally true when dealing with strangers, but almost universally true when relating to family and friends.

Unless someone in your family or friendship circle consistently acts in bad faith or displays sociopathic behavior, give them the benefit of the doubt. If you can't let it go, talk to them. "You know," you might say, "when you do 'this' or say 'that' I feel (not you make me feel, but I feel) disrespected or sad or unloved." Be brave enough and emotionally intelligent enough to have a conversation that focuses on the behavior, not the person. Taking this approach may clear the air and restore emotional balance in the relationship. Ideally, the offending behavior changes. If not, you may choose to modify your reaction, avoid putting yourself in similar situations, or put some distance between yourself and a chronic offender.

The old sayings "Never let the sun go down upon your wrath" or "Don't go to bed angry" are wise, especially in the context of preserving relationships over time. The more openly, honestly, and quickly hurt feelings are addressed, the less likely it is that you'll become one of those people who, for years, hasn't spoken to a sibling or who has lost touch with a former close friend. If you're feeling a sense of loss from a former close relationship, it may not be too late to have that chat now.

Do Unto Others. That's really the bottom line, isn't it? Live by "the Golden Rule" and treat others as you want them to treat you. That's what good conscience dictates. It's hard to go wrong following that path.

Thank you for Reading. May your blessings be many and your troubles few. I wish you and yours a successful and joyful life. My fondest hope is that all your dreams come true, that you get the life you've imagined and live the life you deserve.

YOU DESERVE SUCCESS.
YOU DESERVE HAPPINESS.
YOU DESERVE THE LIFE YOU'VE
IMAGINED.
YOU DESERVE TO MEET YOUR GOALS
AND FULFILL YOUR DREAMS.

I WISH ALL THESE THINGS FOR YOU!
* *

PLEASE KNOW THAT **A REVIEW** WOULD BE
IMMENSELY HELPFUL AND GREATLY
APPRECIATED.
IF YOU HAVE FEEDBACK THAT WOULD
IMPROVE FUTURE VERSIONS OF THIS BOOK OR
BETTER MY SELF-PUBLISHING EFFORTS, I'M
ALL EARS.

PLEASE VISIT MY WEBSITE,
WWW.DELORESCRUM.COM, FOR AN OPPORTUNITY TO
JOIN THE SUCCESS CIRCLE & OTHER OPPORTUNITIES.

WITH GRATITUDE – DELORES CRUM

DELORES@DELORESCURM.COM